JOURNEYS OF DISCOVERY

JOURNEYS OF DISCOVERY

Ancestral Searches in India

Shubha Singh

SHIPRA

ISBN: 978-81-7541-638-3

First Published in India in 2012

Journeys of Discovery: Ancestral Searches in India

Published by:
SHIPRA PUBLICATIONS
H.O.: LG 18-19, Pankaj Central Market, Patparganj,
I.P. Ext., Delhi-110092, Tel: 91-11-2223 5152, 2223 6152
Br.Off.: 4617/18, Ansari Road, Darya Ganj,
New Delhi-110002, Tel: 6594 6453, 9810522367
E-mail: info@shiprapublications.com
www.shiprapublications.com

Contents

Introduction

Indians whose ancestors settled in the colonies of the New World have traditionally displayed strong nostalgic sentiments about the mother country. In the past decade or more, many people of Indian origin have tried to locate their ancestral homes in India. I had known of people from Fiji, Mauritius and the Caribbean islands who had wanted to reconnect their ties with India. But I came to realise the depth of their longing to trace their roots only after I wrote about the experiences of a couple of Indians who had managed to locate and visit homes of their ancestors' in India. I began to receive a regular stream of emails in response to the articles from people of Indian descent, many of them wanted advice and help in carrying out their own family searches. Most of them were descendants of Indians who had gone as indentured workers to the British colonies. But the nostalgic yearnings are not restricted to only this section of the Indian diaspora, the longing to connect is a characteristic of several other groups within the Indian diasporic community.

Ronnie Ramsooroop sent an email after reading the stories of two women's journey to their roots. He wrote: "The article about two women searching for their roots in India was inspiring. I have been wanting to trace my great grandparents' homes in India. My grandmother used to talk about them but I did not pay much heed in my younger days. Unfortunately, my grandmother died three years ago and I do not have much information about where my great grandparents came from. I only remember that my aji said that they came on the ship, Ganges. Can you help me?"

I tried to give Ronnie a few pointers on where to seek more information about the family, based on the one vital clue he had

– the name of the ship his ancestor travelled on. But that was among the first of the several dozens of emails I received on the subject in the next couple of years. I eventually came up with a standard piece of advice for most of the emails – look for the emigration pass (which gave the home address), check in the National Archives for the emigration pass on the basis of name, ship and date of arrival. But quite a few of them did not have this information and I had to work out ways in which they could gather these crucial details. Many of them just wanted to know how others had gone about the search for their ancestral heritage. But what was evident in all the emails was an intense yearning to trace the old links.

I replied to each email, telling them – talk to older relatives; listen to the stories they relate and then write them down. It is these memories that form the history of your family, and it is through them you get to know the lives of your ancestors. I told them about successful searches that I had heard about such as Harish Boodhoo's search.

It was in 1987 that the Antar Rashtriya Sahyog Parishad (ARSP), a non-governmental organisation based in Delhi, carried out a roots search for Harish Boodhoo, who was then the Deputy Prime Minister of Mauritius. Harish Boodhoo provided some information about his paternal grandfather to the ARSP. Shri Baleshwar Agarwal, secretary general of the ARSP and other senior members worked out the general location of the ancestral village in Hazaribagh district, formerly in the state of Bihar but now part of the state of Jharkhand. According to family history as related by Harish Boodhoo, his grandfather was about ten years old when he was kidnapped and sent off to the recruiter's depot. The young lad was crying so bitterly that he could not even give his name to the recruiters. The recruiters jotted the boy's name as Buddhu (fool) and that became the name by which he was known through out his life in Mauritius. His family took on the name Boodhoo as a surname and the name has carried on till it adorned the high office of the deputy prime minister of the country.

In August 1987, Harish Boodhoo, Baleshwar Agarwal and RK Sinha travelled to Patna and then took a car to the nearest *thana* (police station). The village was 10 kms from the *thana*; the party reached the village, hot and dusty from the long drive. The village *mukhiya* (headman) gave them a tall glass of sweet tea which perked them up. The *mukhiya* told them that there was no 'mahto' (Kurmi caste) left in the village, they had all moved to another village, Simatali down the road. There was no *pucca* (tarsealed) road to the next village, so the group began walking along the *kutcha* (dirt) path. After walking for some time, they reached the village where they saw a group of men playing cards. Initially, the villagers were wary of the strangers; they were afraid that the visitors had come to collect payment for something.

It took a little time for the misunderstanding to be cleared up – Harish Boodhoo was a son of the village and he was a high dignitary in far away Mauritius. Harish met some cousins – grandchildren of his grandfather's younger brothers. It was a happy homecoming and it brought joy to the entire village in more ways than one. Sometime after Harish Boodhoo's visit a metalled road was constructed right up to the village, connecting it to the main highway. The road was named after Harish Boodhoo, illustrious son of Simatali village.

The desire to trace one's roots is not restricted to Indians. Genealogy is a thriving business as well as a favourite hobby around the world. As more and more countries receive migrants and embrace multi-culturalism, the new arrivals do not face the same pressures to assimilate in the host culture as did the earlier migrants. Migrants are now even encouraged to celebrate their dual or multiple identities in the host country. Descendants of migrants in many countries display a need to search for their ancestral heritage and it is in America, the land of immigrants where the yearning is at its highest. The tourist trade in Ireland and Scotland has a thriving "roots business" from America, Australia, South Africa and several other countries. On a popular walking tour in Dublin, I noticed just two Indians and two Japanese among a largish group of Americans and Australians of Irish descent soaking in the history of the city. The Chinese have a name for it – *huija* – returning home to the ancestral hometown.

Alex Haley's book, '*Roots: The Saga of an American Family*' is credited with sparking off an interest in searching for one's ancestral heritage. The book was a phenomenal success worldwide when it was published in 1974. It was based on the story of Haley's ancestor, Kunta Kinte who was kidnapped in The Gambia in 1767 and taken on a slave ship to Annapolis, Maryland in the US and sold as a slave. Haley traced his family connection through seven generations to Kunta Kinte in Juffure village.

The book ran into controversies as historians questioned some of Haley's claims about his discovery of Kunta Kinte's village, Juffure in The Gambia, but the book had a powerful impact on the African-American community in the US. It changed the community's self-image, giving it a sense of history beyond the period of enslavement – of belonging to a long cultural heritage.

Alex Haley created a memorial to Kunta Kinte, retracing his journey from his Gambian village to being sold to a plantation owner in Virginia in southern America. The memorial in Annapolis, Maryland still draws about a million visitors a year some four decades after the book was written. The story of *Roots* was converted into a highly popular television mini-series in the 1970s. The tele-series was revived some 25 years later and proved that the story still retained its hold on the audience. The tele-series boosted the interest in genealogy in the US and inspired African Americans to learn more about their ancestry.

Haley later wrote another book, '*Queen*' based on his grandmother, Queen's family history. Queen's mother was the daughter of a female slave, Viney and a white overseer named William Baugh who lived on a plantation in Alabama. Another interesting episode in the Haley saga came up last year when a British newspaper reported that DNA tests had established that Haley had a Scottish ancestor. The website Ancestry.co.uk sought to match a sample of DNA from Chris Haley, nephew of Alex Haley with genetic material from others who had provided their DNA. It matched with June Baff-Black, (Baff is close enough to Baugh), June now lives in Wales and her lineage goes back to 17th century Scotland.

I read the book, *Roots* in 1975 when I was living in Fiji and was drawn by the strong parallels with the indenture system – of a community torn from its homeland, all ties cut off from the family and pushed into servitude in an unfamiliar land. It was about the time when my brother, Ajay Singh was carrying out a family search at the Fiji National Archives about our own ancestors. About our great grandparents, Ram Chandra and Padam Kaur's voyage to Fiji as indentured workers in 1885, their return to Jaingara village in Agra district twenty years later and their son, Bere Singh's return to Fiji to work. It was a fascinating family saga that unfolded through old, musty files. It was immensely interesting for us as my grandfather, Bere Singh had rarely spoken about his sojourn in Fiji.

Three decades later, I could empathise with overseas Indians desire to discover their family histories. I responded to the queries as best as I could till I decided to put together the experiences of other roots seekers. It was not only the third and fourth generation descendants of Indian migrations who are keen to trace their family background, even the children of later day migrants to the developed countries are keen to explore their Indian cultural heritage. Children of migrants to America, Australia, Canada want to know about their family origins and what makes them Indian.

A young American of Indian origin, Sivaraman explained the pull India exerted on his mind and emotions. Sivaraman said:

"When I was growing up in America, my parents rarely talked about the past. There is a mode of exile that dwells on everything that was lost – the house with the mango tree, crisp winter mornings and the monsoon clouds. But, as a child I heard only fragments of our family history from my father. I did not feel a strong tie to India when I was growing up, but I knew I was from Vijayawada. One day I sat down with my father and asked him to tell me everything he knew about our family history. He told me about our family's rise from humble origins. He described how my grandfather went to Singapore to work to earn money to pay off the family debts and how the family scraped together the funds to send my father to America. I spoke to my father's brothers and sister; their memories were slightly different from my father's. I knew I had to travel to India to see for myself the home they left behind."

Many people of Indian descent do not have any information about their ancestors' origins. Often the migrants were too busy trying to make a success in the new land that they had little time to think or talk about the old days. There is little to connect their descendants to their Indian heritage except for their Indian ethnicity and Indian values, and the family narratives of the voyage from India to an alien place and lifestyle. But they still want to travel to India and visit the places associated with their ancestors in the ancestral homeland. They want to read about experiences similar to those their ancestors went through. This is my effort to put together the experiences of people tracing their roots in India for those who are unable to search for their roots or are starting out on their family search.

Migration, Indenture, Dislocation, Identity

Migration is a timeless process – men, women and children have moved with their livestock in search of new pastures and more fertile farmland since ancient times. People have migrated to new places through the ages looking for better opportunities. The migrants have carried with them melancholic sagas and epics of the lost homeland. The nostalgia for the original homeland has been handed down through the generations through songs and legends.

In ancient times, Indians migrated as traders, monks, artisans and adventure-seekers. In latter years they went abroad to work as farm labour, as industrial workers; as merchants and entrepreneurs, as teachers, doctors, and engineers; skilled and semi-skilled workers to countries around the world. People of Indian origin living beyond Indian shores are estimated to number 25 million and live in 189 countries. Spread around the world, from America to Argentina, from Malaysia to Madagascar, Indians have migrated in search of new opportunities and prospered in their adopted homelands. A majority of these overseas or *pravasi* Indians retain some connection to India whether they are recent migrants or fourth generation descendants of migrants.

Contrary to the popular belief that Indians were reluctant to cross the seas (*kala pani*) for fear of caste defilement, Indians were avid travellers to distant places for centuries. Ancient ties linked India to the Hindu kingdoms of South-East Asia, Buddhist monks went to East Asia and Central Asia, merchants regularly crossed the Indian Ocean to trade in North and East Africa and further afield. But regular, organised migration from India began only in the 19th century when Indians were taken to the British colonies to work on the sugar cane plantations under the indenture system. Over one million indentured Indians were taken to Mauritius, the Caribbean, Fiji, South Africa and the French and Dutch imperial colonies of Reunion, Guadeloupe and Suriname from the 19th century to the early years of the 20th century.

The Indian diasporic community has to a large extent retained its links with India and their cultural traditions. For many whose ancestors left India several generations ago, the connection may be as tenuous as the use of a few words or phrases associated with an Indian language, some exotic spices added to a favourite dish, the choice of vivid colours that evoke Indian textiles or a special recipe used for festive occasions. Others have recreated the language and practices and rituals of the homeland in their new milieu. Even to those who have little to do with India and whose Indianness has been diluted through time, the link may lie dormant but is still extant.

In countries that have a large ethnic migrant minority, the minority community is usually able to retain many of the symbols and attributes of its ethnic identity as the Indians did in Mauritius, Fiji and South Africa. It is the new migrant who is expected to quickly assimilate into the host society. America advocated the 'melting pot' concept of assimilation for new arrivals, France expected the migrant to completely merge into the French lifestyle and culture. But multi-ethnic societies like Canada, Britain and America have since moved from ignoring migrant cultures to consciously celebrating the different ethnic cultures existing within their population. These countries are encouraging their minorities to retain their ethnic attributes within the larger value system of the host society as well as retain links with the mother country.

As America's multi-cultural character has got more varied it has encouraged the young generation to be more aware of and to explore their cultural heritage. For the immigrant and especially second generation migrant, there is also a need for re-evaluating ethnic identity. Migrant groups absorb influences of the host society as they seek to assimilate in it. These influences recreate the migrants into an identifiable group that carries the attributes of both host and mother societies; some bits of both societies that go to create a new group.

A back to roots movement has caught on in the world. Migrants and their children are keen to stay in touch with the old country. At the same time, genealogy has grown into a popular pastime around the world, especially in countries which have received large numbers of migrants. Books like *Roots* by Alex Haley and television series such as the BBC series – *Who do you think you are?* – that traced the family histories of studio guests became hugely popular and set off a trend of family searches. And more and more readers have become interested in the past, especially their own family's past – to look for their roots. Americans are travelling through Germany and Poland to look for places connected with their ancestors' lives before they migrated to the US. The Irish diaspora is a significant source of tourists for Ireland. Shinto priests hold upto 15 festivals a year to welcome overseas Japanese pilgrims to Taisho in Japan. Cheaper travel has accelerated such "homecomings" in most diasporas.

Amy Tan, the Chinese American author of the best selling novel, '*The Joy Luck Club*', remarked while on a visit to China, "As soon as my feet touched China, I felt Chinese." Many people of Indian descent express similar sentiments when they visit India. French philosopher, Simeon Weil wrote in *The Need for Roots*, that "perhaps the most important and least recognised need of the human soul was the need to be rooted." Roots provide stability and nourishment while the social and cultural structure is the soil that sustains and anchors them.

Australia-born Dharmesh Chand's daughter came back from school one day and asked about the family history for a school project.

It started Dharmesh thinking, he realised that he knew very little about his grandparents. Why did they decide to migrate to Fiji? How did the family of sugarcane farmers decide to send their eldest son – his father – to study in Australia? These nagging questions led him to embark on a journey to search for his origins. A year later he travelled to a small village in Basti district. The old house had fallen down, the family had moved away, but Dharmesh was deeply moved as he walked around the village where his grandfather was born. "It gave me a sense of history, of my family's origins," he said.

Migration

The first organised stream of migration from India began in the 19th century with the indenture system, when Indian workers were taken to the plantation colonies to meet the shortage of labour. In a period of about a hundred years, from 1835 to 1916 just over 1.19 million men, women and children were transported to about 19 colonies to work. A majority of these migrants stayed on in the colonies and only about a third of the migrants returned home to India. Aside from the indenture migration to the imperial colonies, Indians migrated to the Straits Settlements, Burma, Malaya and Ceylon, either as individual fare paying passengers or under the *kangani* system. Under the *kangani* system, a contractor hired a group of workers, usually from the same group of villages and took them to work in Ceylon and Malaya. From mid 19th century onwards there was a steady flow of Indian migrants who went as far as Hong Kong, China, Central Asia, Russia and Japan to look for work. Indian convicts were taken to Singapore for construction of the newly established trading post and within a few decades, Indians had formed the second largest community in Singapore. Indians are now about 7 per cent of the population of Singapore. From 1880s onwards a regular stream of adventurous young men set off from the villages of Punjab to look for work in foreign lands.

Another wave of Indian migration took place when Indians were taken to East Africa to build the cross African railway that connected Mombasa on the coast of Kenya to Kampala in Uganda. An army of service providers accompanied the railroad workers, to cater to their needs as cooks, laundry workers, peddlers, traders etc. Many of them stayed on in Africa after the railroad construction was over. They were joined by a stream of migrants who came looking for better economic opportunities in the new East African territories. Enterprising Gujarati and Sindhi traders moved across the world to trade, and many of them found work in East Africa. The years after World War I saw a spurt in migration, especially by former soldiers of the British India forces.

Indians moved to Britain in the 1950s to take up jobs in the post-World War II burst of reconstruction work in the country. In later years, streams of men and women from Punjab and other places went to Britain to work in the textile mills and most of them did not return to their villages in India. Later, the oil price boom and the soaring profits of the 1970s in the Gulf countries opened up yet another region for migration and thousands of Indians went to work at the new developmental projects coming up in the oil rich countries. Indians now form the largest expatriate community in the Persian Gulf countries. Towards the end of the 1970s, America, Canada, Australia and later New Zealand lifted their immigration restrictions against Asians, allowing Indians to enter their countries. In the past two decades, Indian professionals have moved across to different parts of the world. Thus did Indians spread across the globe.

People have a deep-seated need to know where they come from, what makes them who they are, and whom they take after. The nostalgic draw of learning about family origins can become a passion for some searchers. Many are moved to tears as they learn of the experiences that their parents and grandparents went through. Visits to the places associated with their ancestors help them to become aware of their ethnic heritage as people of Indian descent, and to build their own cultural identities. It helps them to understand India and the Indian people.

The number of Indo-Guyanese wanting to search family history is much more than Indians in the other Caribbean islands. One of the main reasons is that there has been large scale migration by Indo-Guyanese from Guyana over several decades because of the difficult living conditions under an autocratic regime. Most of the Indo-Guyanese migrated to America and Canada and their ties with Guyana were weakened. The younger generation of Indo-Guyanese in Canada have a more difficult time over questions of identity because the two time migrations have cut them off from their Indo-Guyanese background. Therefore they feel the need to search for the Indian part of their ethnic identity.

Indenture

Indenture was a form of labour contract in use in Britain in the 16th and 17th century. The term indenture referred to indentations or marks made on a contract as a means of identification by illiterate workers. In the days when workers could not read or write, the indentation or the marking was the way through which they could identify their contracts. Two copies of the contract were placed one on top of the other, and both were marked by tearing off a corner or making indentations that could be recognised by the worker. This was meant to protect him from an unscrupulous master who could make changes in the contracts.

When the new colonies were being settled in America, young men and women were brought over from Europe and Britain as indentured workers. They were brought to work on the tobacco plantations in Virginia and Maryland. Young men and women would sign an indenture contract in lieu of their sea passage to the New World. The servant would work for his board and lodging for a period of four to seven years for the master, who was allowed to loan or sell the indentured worker to another master.

The conditions of the indentured workers were quite akin to slaves during the contract period. The master had the right to beat the servant, penalize him for mistakes and for not completing the work set for him; he could even have his indenture period extended as a penalty. At the end of the contract period, the servant was to be given a year's supply of corn, two sets of clothes, and the tools necessary for him to ply his trade.

It was a time when there was high level of unemployment in England while there was need for large number of workers to clear the land for planting tobacco and tending to the fields in America. Women indentured servants were required for household duties, dairy work, laundry etc. Thousands of migrants reached the American shores as indentured servants. The treatment of indentured servants depended on individual masters – the masters controlled the lives of their servants, and while some masters were good employers, many were not.

During the 16th and 17th century, Europeans were taken to the Caribbean islands as indentured workers. By mid 1600s the number of indentured servants began declining as unemployment was no longer as high in Europe and Britain and plantation owners turned to using slaves brought in from Africa.

Slavery in the British territories was abolished in 1830s after a long public campaign, but it led to a drastic labour shortage in the colonies. The freed slaves moved off the plantations or demanded better wages and conditions to work on the cane fields. The production of sugarcane plummeted and the plantation owners put pressure on the British government for a fresh supply of workers. Sugar was "king" as it was referred to in those days in the plantation colonies. It was the mainstay of the economy in the islands so it became imperative to find new workers to grow the sugarcane.

It was deemed necessary to have some amount of control over the workers as work on the plantations was hard. Indenture contracts bound the worker to work for the plantation owner he or she was assigned to. India and China were the two countries with a substantial population with sound knowledge of agricultural work and the two countries became the main sources for labour for the colonies. Following the pressure from the colonies, the British government allowed workers to be imported from India to work in the sugar producing colonies on indentured contracts.

The first group of Indian workers were sent to Mauritius in 1834, but by 1838 the British government had stopped the emigration because of the rampant abuse of the workers. The government constituted a committee in Calcutta to go into allegations of mistreatment and abuse. A new regulated system of migration was instituted with appropriate safeguards with emigration agents and a Protector of Immigrants to oversee the recruitment of workers. In 1842 emigration to Mauritius was re-opened. Emigration to Trinidad, British Guiana and Jamaica was started in 1844 while Grenada and St Lucia were allowed to import workers from 1856 and 1858. From 1860 onwards, Natal was allowed to import Indian indentured workers to work in the mines and the plantations.

The French colonies were also bringing in Indian workers but the workers in the French territories had few safeguards. In 1860, the British government had signed an agreement for the importation of Indian workers to the French territories of Reunion Island, Guadeloupe, Martinique and French Guiana. By 1872 the British allowed Indian workers to be taken to the Dutch colony of Surinam and St Croix. Indenture migration to Fiji began in 1879 shortly after the islands were annexed by the British crown. However, emigration to the French colonies was stopped in the 1880s after persistent complaints of ill-treatment and abuse of the workers.

There was a qualitative difference in the system of indentured workers who were taken to America or Australia and the indenture system as it operated in the Caribbean, Mauritius and Fiji. The Indian workers were lodged in the same barracks that had housed the slaves on the plantation estates and the supervisors and managers carried over many of the practices that they had used with the slaves. The racial difference between the employer, the supervisor and the worker added a new dimension to the labour dynamics leading to much abuse of the workers.

When they arrived in the colonies, the Indian workers were despised and oppressed – their religious beliefs and practices, their different languages were ridiculed. They were categorised as "the lowest and least desirable elements" from the lowest castes – in order to maintain the so-called superiority of the white man and justify the harsh treatment meted out to them. They were portrayed as men who were used to that kind of handling and only responded to harsh treatment.

The indentured immigrants were mainly from rural backgrounds, with only a small leavening of town folk fallen on bad times or looking for better opportunities. The widely accepted image of indentured workers was that they belonged to the disadvantaged sections of Indian society, those at the bottom of the social scale. But more rational studies of the immigrants' backgrounds have shown that the indentured workers were a cross section of the Indian rural population. They were farmers, artisans, potters, cobblers and boatmen. There were some brahmins and thakurs, though brahmins were not preferred as they could not do hard, manual work.

Hugh Tinker records in '*A New System of Slavery: The Export of Indian Labour Overseas, 1830-1920*'[1] that the ship Medea arrived in British Guiana with '13 agricultural labourers, with one lime-burner, one cowherd, three peons and a sweeper who made up the list of those accustomed to outdoor labour; the remaining 14 were priests, weavers, scribes, shoemakers, beggars and so forth'. Another emigration report for Suriname stated that the majority of the migrants had 'formerly been house servants, soldiers, policemen, barbers, shopkeepers, hawkers, etc.'

In the early decades of indenture the main districts of recruitment were Benares, Azamgarh, Gorakhpur, Jaunpur, Muzaffarpur, Champaran, Shahabad, Patna and Gaya. Later migration concentrated in the districts of Faizabad, Basti and Gonda. As recruitment centres were opened in Agra and other northern cities, migration from western Uttar Pradesh, Punjab, and parts of Rajasthan picked up. When the indenture ships began sailing from Madras port, recruiters brought in migrants from the coastal and interior districts of Tamil Nadu and Andhra Pradesh.

One of the important reasons for the push for emigration in India was the difficult conditions in the rural areas. The lack of employment opportunities in urban areas was another reason for migration. The rural distress was partly due to colonial policies. The colonial administration made significant changes in the land revenue and ownership patterns in north India, thousands of large estates were confiscated and the tenant farmers displaced. The Indian Uprising in 1857 was followed by executions and confiscations of land from owners in the regions that had revolted against British imperialism. Many people had to flee or were forcibly displaced from their land-holdings – the turmoil in the rural areas continued for several years.

During the Mughal period and earlier ages, farm land was not a commodity that could be sold as there was no concept of individual ownership. Peasant cultivators had a hereditary right to cultivate the land and they paid revenue based on the harvest to the revenue collector. The British changed the pattern of land ownership and revenue collection; land grants were given to the *zamindars* (land lords) with titles that allowed them the right to sell the land. Land acquired a saleable value. The cultivator-peasant was turned into a lease-holder who could be evicted for failure to pay the land revenue. Rates had to be paid in cash instead of a fixed share in the harvest. A fixed portion of produce of the land meant that the farmer could withstand a poor harvest due to scanty rainfall or pest attack. Cash payment, however meant that the farmer had to find the money to pay the land revenue even if the crop had failed. Farmers had to borrow to pay the land revenue, especially during poor harvests, which led to mounting debts and eviction from the land. The increasing cultivation of cash crops added to the rural distress in times of drought. Farmers were made to grow cash crops like cotton and opium which left them without a stock of food grain or rice to feed the family till the next crop was harvested. The new land system disrupted the basis of rural society in India which existed through rights and obligations between different sections of society – between the zamindar, the farmer, the artisan, the potter, the leather worker etc. People were forced to move to the towns to look for work. This provided a pool of people for recruiting indentured workers for the colonies.

The first group of Indians to migrate under a system of government regulation went to the French held territory, Reunion Island in the mid 1820s. Most of them travelled from the French enclaves of Pondicherry and Karikal on the eastern coast of India. By the 1840s the legislation for export of labour from India was enacted and emigration was allowed from the port of Calcutta, followed by Madras and then later from Bombay.

The indenture period was for five years, after which the worker was released from his employment and could find work elsewhere or pay for his passage to India. After ten years of residence in the colony, the workers were entitled to a free passage back to India. The indenture period came to be known as '*girmit*' by the indentured workers from the indenture agreement or contract they signed, mostly with a thumb impression. The indentured workers came to be called '*girmitiyas*'.

Under the terms and conditions of the indenture contract, the workers were bound to work for nine hours a day through five and a half days a week. Employers were to provide accommodation and medical care, and rations for the first six months. Work was assigned according to task, which meant that the day's work ended only after the allotted task was completed. It often meant that the work period extended beyond nine hours depending on the whims of the supervisor or the employer's desire to extract more work. Adult males (15 years and above) were paid one shilling per day in Fiji, while women received nine pence for doing three-fourth's of a man's task per day.

The government in Calcutta (which was then the capital of the British administration) appointed a Protector of Emigrants and each colonial government wishing to import indentured labour appointed an Emigration Agent. The Emigration Agent hired recruiters who had to be licensed by the Protector of Emigrants. The licensed recruiters in turn hired local men who were known as '*arkatis*' to locate prospective emigrants. It was a system that was open to a great deal of abuse. The *arkatis* used various means to entice emigrants; deception and exaggeration were a stock in trade, especially since people were not willing to go far from their homes. The *arkatis* were usually local men and women, whose areas of operation were the small towns and pilgrimage spots. The *arkatis* were reluctant to go to the rural areas for recruitment since the indenture migration was strongly disliked by the villagers and the *arkatis* were likely to get beaten up if they were caught by the village folk. The local police and the district officials also discouraged potential recruits from migrating. The *arkatis* usual haunt was the local fairs, the *haats* (markets), and temples, places of pilgrimage and railway stations. These were the places where it was easy to approach people. The *arkatis* kept a watch out for the newcomer to town, the poor and distressed, and the naive and uncertain individual who would welcome advice offered by a friendly local who spoke persuasively and with an air of authority. *Arkatis* looked out for young men and women who seemed to have run away from home or had lost their way. A drought or a series of poor harvests would make it easier to recruit migrants for the colonies. People in the rural area had begun to move out of their villages to go to the nearest town to look for work. The *arkatis* wove glowing pictures of a comfortable life and plentiful land that was available to the migrant, to inveigle the unsuspecting recruit.When they accepted the rosy offer of the *arkati*, most of the men and women were ignorant of the actual place they were destined for, the length of the voyage and the kind of conditions they would encounter on arrival. The immigrants were told by the *arkatis* that the place they were going to was not far, and implied that it was part of India. Mauritius was called *Mirch desh*, Trinidad was *Chini Dad*, Suriname was known as *Sri Ram* and Demerara came to be known as *Damraila*. Many workers did not realise that they were going overseas till they reached Calcutta.

Recruitment

Girmitiya accounts speak of '*dhoka*' (deception) by the recruiters and there is a popular belief that the indentured workers were duped, tricked, even kidnapped into servitude. While there were instances of deception and use of force, such as Totaram Sanadhaya faced at the depot, the majority of the illiterate migrants were ignorant of the actual terms of the contract they signed. Those who changed their mind about migrating where threatened with jail if they failed to pay for their board and lodging, forcing them to acquiesce to the *arkati's* plans. However, there were a number of instances when prospective migrants left the depot on their own and many others who were rejected during the medical examination.

People from Punjab were promised that they would be given jobs as security guards and in the police. In one incident in Fiji a group of Punjabis refused to do the work allotted to them on the plantation, claiming that they had been promised jobs as guards. The Punjabis revolted but their revolt was put down forcefully and the group was scattered to different locations.

Some indentured workers had been coerced or tricked into accepting the indenture contract, but in most cases it was misrepresentation of the indenture conditions, fanciful tales of the kind of life they would have in the colonies and in very many cases it was concealing the fact that the place they were being sent to was not within India.

Munshi Rehman Khan and Totaram Sanadhaya were two *girmitiyas* who related their experience of recruitment in their memoirs. Munshi Rehman Khan, an indentured worker in Suriname wrote of his experience with the *arkati* in his autobiography called '*Jeevan Prakash*' based on the daily diary he wrote throughout his life. According to the English translation of *Jeevan Prakash* [2] by Kathinka Sinha-Kerkhoff, Ellen Bal and Alok Deo Singh, Munshi Rahman Khan was renowned for his knowledge of the Ramayana and was often called for recitals. He was a prolific writer and was knighted by Queen Juliana of the Netherlands in 1951 for his literary work.

Munshi Rahman Khan was born in Hamirpur district of the United Provinces, his family lived in comfortable circumstances as his father was an assistant to the zamindar. He was educated but was a restless boy and ran away from home once; after he completed his middle school he got a job as a school teacher (*munshi*). A visit to Kanpur to see the *Ramlila* led to a fateful meeting that resulted in his sailing off to the Dutch colony of Suriname in 1898. Munshi Rahman Khan was a remarkable man. He sailed to the Dutch colony on the ship, Avon. He worked in a plantation as an indentured worker, and then bought some land and began farming on his own. He stayed in touch with his relatives in India, and even sent them some money over the years.

Munshi Rahman Khan related in detail his meeting with the *arkati*. He was standing near the bazaar, when two Muslim men came by; he greeted them since they looked respectable though he had his doubts about them. When he told them that he was to catch the 8 o' clock train to Chandpur, they promptly said that the train had been rescheduled for later in the day. As they got talking the two men asked whether he was interested in a job. They said that it was a government job. "Then they asked, 'Are you educated?' I said, 'Yes. I have passed the middle school'. The men happily told me, 'Then you could become a *sirdar* (headman) and receive a salary of 12 *annas* per day. The work has to do with sugar, there you will have to supervise the labourers and travel on the government's boat."

Munshi Rahman Khan was attracted by the offer, 12 annas a day was a good sum of money. The *arkatis* told him: 'The ship from Calcutta takes three months to reach *Sriram tapu*. If you are doubtful about your salary, then come with us and we will get you registered in the government office. Come now and we will show you those labourers whom you will have to supervise. From today the government will pay for all your expenses.' They crossed the canal and went to the depot of Babu Ram Narain Singh. They took Rahman Khan into the courtyard and showed him the newly recruited men and women and said, 'Please see all these people, they will be going with you.' The *arkatis* disappeared after some time and then Babu Ram Narain Singh told him to stay in the courtyard and in his absence keep a watch on all the recruits. The bird was trapped and caged, Rahman Khan wrote. "If only I would have had the guts to cancel my agreement in front of the Magistrate, I could have come out of that mess. But I did not know of this possibility but even if I had known I would still have remained there because the Great Allah had picked me out and I was destined to leave Hindustan and earn a living in Suriname. It was sad, very sad." Even the educated and well-off Munshi could not extract himself out of the web cast by the *arkatis*.

Totaram Sanadhya went to Fiji Islands as an indentured worker in 1993, when he returned to India he wrote a book on his experiences in Fiji called '*Fiji dwip mei mere ekkis varsh*' (My twenty-one years in Fiji Islands)[3] . In Fiji, Totaram Sanadhaya became a respected leader of the community, he organised the Sanathan Dharam Sabha in Fiji and corresponded with the Indian freedom fighter, Gopal Krishna Gokhale and Mahatma Gandhi regarding the travails of the Indian indentured labour.

His book painted a graphic picture of the conditions in Fiji. The book was widely circulated in the country and helped arouse public opinion in India against the indenture system. On his return to India Totaram Sanadhya travelled through the country and lectured against the indenture system. Towards the later stage of his life he went to live at Sabarmati Ashram; Mahatma Gandhi wrote about Totaram Sanadhya that he "was an ornament to the Sabarmati Ashram. He was not a scholar but he was wise." Totaram Sanadhya was a *brahmin* by birth, but his emigration form listed him as a *thakur*. *Brahmins* were not favoured as migrant workers since the colonial authorities wanted farm workers. Several *brahmins* concealed their castes or their recruiters concealed their castes in order to add them on the list of migrants. Totaram Sanadhya belonged to Hirangaon village in Firozabad district of Uttar Pradesh. His father had died at a young age and the family had to struggle to survive in the village. He was 17 years old when he left the village to look for work. Totaram Sanadhya wrote in his book of how he met a man near the market who asked him if he was looking for work. The story he relates in his book is similar to several hundred other such cases of recruitment by the *arkatis*. Totaram replied that he was willing to work for a year and the *arakati* persuaded him to come with him promising him work in a very pleasant place. The *arkati* took Totaram to a house where about a hundred other men and almost sixty women were present. The men and women were seated in two queues and were eating their dinner. Three days later the group of men and women were prepared to appear before a magistrate at the courthouse. The *arkati* coached the men and women to say 'yes' to every question the magistrate asked them or the *arkati* threatened that the official would send them to jail. As the prospective migrants were presented before the magistrate, the official asked them: "are you prepared to go to Fiji Islands?" to which the migrant obediently replied "yes". The magistrate did not ask whether the migrant knew where Fiji was or whether he understood the terms and conditions of the contract. The magistrate cleared 165 people within 20 minutes, Totaram Sanadhya wrote. The group was taken by train to Calcutta; from Howrah station they were taken to the depot. At the depot the Emigration Agent told the group that they were going to Fiji and would get 12 *annas* a day for working on the fields. They would work for five years and then return to India after paying for their passage.

Totaram Sanadhya did not want to go away for five years. He asked to be allowed to go and look for his elder brother who was in Calcutta, but was not allowed to leave the depot. He was locked up in a room without food and water till he agreed to go to Fiji. The migrants went through a medical examination where a doctor checked whether they were fit for farm work. The migrants then waited for a ship to arrive and begin their journey to Fiji. It took three months and 12 days for the ship and its migrant passengers to reach Fiji Islands. Totaram Sanadhya returned to India after 21 years. The Protector of Emigrants was responsible for ensuring that the emigration agents followed the regulations. He had to inspect the ship for being seaworthy and that the emigrants were going on their own volition. The ship sailed only after the ship's captain received a certificate from the Protector of Emigrants. However, the system was still open to misuse and manipulation.

Dislocation

The passage on the ship was the final break with the past life. In the cramped quarters of the ship, the migrants had to face up to the new rules and practices that would govern their lives. Caste barriers and traditional values broke down as the migrants ate from a communal kitchen. It came as a shock to the migrants and there were some who tried to jump off the ship as they realised the enormity of the decision they had taken. It became usual practice for a small boat to accompany the indenture ship as it set sail from Calcutta port down the Hooghly River to the Bay of Bengal, its job was to pick up anyone who threw himself off the ship in despair. The long passage on the ship was a time when new bonds of friendship were forged. The ties between ship mates replaced the bonds of blood and family, and they became '*jahaji bhai*' (brothers of the ship). It was a bond that remained through out their lives, with the *jahajis* taking the place of the relatives left behind.

On arrival at the colony, the migrants were kept in quarantine and then allotted to different plantations. The indentured workers were made to stay in the old, cramped barracks left over from the time of slavery with little privacy and sanitation. The system was a degrading one, especially as the safeguards instituted by the Indian government did not work satisfactorily in the colonies. Plantation life was a world of its own, with its own rules and customs, many of which were derived from the days of slavery. It was servitude for a period of five years, but those were five difficult years because of over-tasking, shortfall in payment, punitive punishments that involved cut in wages, physical punishment and even increasing the indenture period. The supervisory staff and the Indian overseers were often brutal in their behaviour and complaints to the civilian authorities did not serve any purpose. Living conditions were poor and the workers suffered from malnutrition, hookworm infestation, anaemia, dysentery and other infectious diseases.

Conditions on the plantations differed from estate to estate, depending on the managers and supervisors. Life could be brutal on a plantation with arbitrary punishments, violence against the men and women, over-tasking and docking of wages. The cramped, unsanitary conditions and lack of medical attention to treating the new diseases added to make indenture hell or "*narak*" as the *girimtiyas* called it. The number of complaints, court cases and the high suicide figures for indentured workers in Fiji testified to the appalling conditions on some of the plantations.

Under government regulations each indenture ship had to carry a passenger load of 40 per cent women. The lives of the women indentured labourers were particularly hard. Women worked in the cane fields, and also looked after the housework when they came back from the cane fields. They also had to protect themselves from the powerful men around them. Among the women immigrants were young widows escaping the harsh restrictions enforced on them by their relatives or those entirely dependent on the mercy of relatives who had little for themselves. There were women who had been abducted or coerced in some manner, or women who had got lost while on a family pilgrimage – it was difficult for such women to return to their homes. There were some who considered indentured migration a way to provide for their small children. More than a third of the women travelled with their family members; some came with their husbands and children and a few came with elder brothers and their families. Some women were widows who migrated with their children; others came alone and got married at the depots while waiting for the ship to take them overseas.

As the indentured labourers fell into the rhythm of life in the sugarcane plantations, they began to take up their traditional vocations during their free time, such as priests, barbers, cobblers, tin workers etc. They kept poultry and grew vegetables. Some who had a bit of money lent it out on interest. It was those who were fortunate enough to become *sirdars* (headmen) on the plantation who had a regular wage instead of being paid according to tasks done. *Sirdars* could be exploitative, for they assigned the daily tasks to the workers. Many *sirdars* extracted small gifts of eggs and vegetables, and even cash from the workers. A few would abuse their positions to take a cut from the daily wages of the workers; they would then lend money at high interest rates to the workers.

In the five years they spent on a plantation, the Indian workers tried to recreate some of the familiar practices. Workers spoke different Indian languages and dialects and a plantation patois evolved that was largely a mix of Bhojpuri and other dialects of north India. Listening to a *bhajan mandali* (hymn singers) or the Ramayana being recited was a favourite pastime. On Sundays, *haats* or markets would be set up and wresting matches would be organised.

On the completion of the indenture contract, the worker received a certificate that made them freemen again. Only about 20 per cent of the former indentured workers signed for a second indenture term, most of them had very little savings and were unsure of starting on their own; others were not able to find a means of earning their livelihood. In Suriname, workers who signed up for the second time got 20 guilders as bonus for each extra year. Those who did not sign the contract were given land on lease or payment and those who gave up their right to a free passage back to India were given 100 guilders.

Indenture was hard labour but it had one mitigating factor; it came to an end after five years. It was something to look forward to, to take the edge away from despair. One day the indenture term would come to an end; and the immigrants had to look for a way to earn their own living. Some workers managed to save, especially if they attained a position of responsibility like sirdar, driver or carpenter. A few made money through gambling, some others through money lending.

Land was available for cultivation in the Caribbean and the Indian migrants drained the swamplands along the coastal areas in Demerara and Suriname to set up farms, while in Trinidad the migrants moved up from the fertile plains into the hilly areas to farm. People took up the occupations they were familiar with as barbers, cobblers, market gardeners, dairymen and security guards. As they settled into living in the colonies, there was the need to form a community and put the travails of *girmit* behind them.

The Indians found different kinds of work; many struggled to earn a living while a few prospered either through their native wit, hard work or some sharp practices. Some migrants sent money back home to their families. The Natal Government Savings Bank increased its Indian deposits from £2800 in 1885 to £23,300 in 1900, while postal remittances went up from £580 per year to £1854 during the same period. (figures cited by Thomas R Metcalf in the chapter on *Indian Minorities in South Africa*,in *Studies in Migration* edited by MSA Rao)

By the later part of the 19th century, there was an awareness of the indenture migration in the rural areas, partly created by letters written by migrants to the relatives back home, some even sent money home and by the trickle of migrants who returned home after completing their indenture contract. The returnees usually gave glowing reports of their sojourn in the islands. There were many family groups who migrated together and the shipping registers recorded a number of men who had re-indentured themselves.

Towards the end of the 19th century, sugar prices were at their lowest, and conditions on the sugarcane plantations deteriorated. Cane growing countries still sought Indian labour but the opposition to the indenture system was growing in India. Indian publications carried reports and letters by missionaries and other public figures like Reverend CF Andrews about the distressing conditions of the indentured workers. First hand accounts of indenture such as Totaram Sanadhaya's '*Fiji Mein Mere Ekees Varsh*' aroused public opinion in India. Indian nationalists like Gopal Krishna Gokhale had moved a resolution in the Legislative Council calling for a ban on indenture. After his return to India from South Africa, Mahatma Gandhi campaigned for the abolition of the indenture system. The campaign became a part of the freedom struggle in India. With mounting opposition in India and among liberal sections in Britain, the colonial government finally stopped indenture recruitment in 1916.

Indenture was a period of intense dislocation – the indentured workers were dislocated from familiar surroundings and taken thousands of miles away to distant lands. They were cut off from friends, family and country and forced into a period of servitude. The pain of separation and the humiliations of indenture added to the sense of dislocation. The *girmitiyas* remained cut off from their relatives in India. Many had left under strained circumstances and the majority were not literate so writing letters could not be the means of restoring the family ties. Also, the end of indenture meant a long period of hard work to make a living in the new country.

As their lives stabilised they found ways to reconstruct their way of life, the *girmitiyas* built their homes and recreated Indian village lifestyles with the old rituals, traditions and festivals. But despite the passage of time, nostalgia for the homeland and memories of India haunted them. Many of them felt a deep sense of guilt and pain at having left their loved ones in the village homes. That nostalgia and longing had an impact on their children and grandchildren. India remained the imagined homeland – the land of their ancestors, the land of the sacred places.

The Indian presence made the colonial societies pluralistic, but the hankering back to India made the community suspect in the eyes of the rest of the colonial society. After Independence, when India was no longer part of the British colonies, the colonial establishment suspected the allegiance of the Indians. It created a distance from India. Town Clerk of Ba town in Fiji, Rajendra Prasad wrote about his apprehensions of travelling in India due to the "unsafe conditions".

After a trip to India, Gaiutra Bahadur wrote an evocative article in the Philadelphia Inquirer (Jan 2004) titled *'Tangled Roots; An American in India: Tourist, seeker, rebel and freak'*. Gauitra wrote that her great-grandmother left India in 1903 from the port of Calcutta for the sugar plantations in Guyana. She was born in that former colony in South America and grew up in Jersey City, N.J., which she described as a scrappy city with a view of the Manhattan skyline. "After all, India had woven, from the distance of a century and nearly 10,000 miles, the cocoon I was raised in. It had warmed our New Jersey apartment with cumin-spiced split pea soup on Sunday mornings and the sweet crooning of its soundtrack diva, Lata Mangeshkar. It had tucked pictures of Ganesh, the god with the elephant trunk, in our bedroom closet. But once I finally was in India, that intimacy became something much more complicated. The land of my forefathers shook my sense of self as though tectonic plates were smashing against each other, in the uncertain territory under the surface of my brown skin," Gauitra wrote.

Identity

Multiculturalism in modern societies has, in some ways, served to emphasise the separate ethnic identity. The question of identity is one that keeps reoccurring in the narrative of Indians living in a multicultural society, or whose families are twice migrants, having moved from one country of migration to another. 'Where are you from?' – is a commonly asked question around the world.

In India it can often be a conversation opener, but for some people it triggers off discomfiting questions of ethnicity and identity. It is a question that many people have struggled to answer. For anyone growing up as a second generation migrant, anyone who has moved from one country to another, from one cultural milieu to another or is part of a newly multicultural society, the question can seem a loaded one relating to issues of inclusion and ethnicity.

Well travelled journalist, Monita Rajpal wrote on her blog that one question she often gets asked is, "where are you from?" She has to think about how to answer that question and each time she wonders whether to give the short answer or the long one. The short answer would be to say I'm Indian, she wrote. But the problem is that she has never lived in India. The long answer would be that she was born in Hong Kong, has lived in Canada, the United States and Britain and believes that all these places have shaped who she is and how she thinks. Monita believes that ancestral history lays the groundwork for defining who we are but who we become has a lot to do with where we grown up and live. She is still searching for the best way to answer the question.

In 2008, I interviewed two young women of Indian origin, who spoke on the subject of ethnic identity; both of them referred to this oft repeated question and their reaction to it. Coincidentally, both the young women were from Canada and were travelling through India to carry out academic research and also to look for their own family links. And it was variations of this question that started them thinking about their ethnic identities and eventually begin searching their family histories.

Alia Somani lived in Canada and was often asked where she came from since she was quite visibly not part of the majority white population. Even when she replied that she was Canadian born, she was sometimes asked 'where are you *really* from?' It was probably an innocuous question, but it set Alia thinking about what it was that set her apart from the normal Canadian teenager. Canada is a country that takes pride in its multicultural society. But its multiculturalism tends to mark out communities as 'visible minorities' in the midst of the majority white, Anglo-Saxon population. This can evoke a feeling of being marked out as 'the other'. It made Alia want to know more about her ethnic and cultural background; to learn about her family's journey to Canada.

Nalini Mohabir was born in Canada and knew little about her family's links to India. Nalini said, "I grew up in Canada, I knew that I had a connection to Guyana. I had vivid memories of meeting aunts, uncles and lots of cousins during visits to Guyana, but I had little idea of my connection to India. But in Canada I was seen as an Indo-Canadian. As I grew up I wanted to know how I was connected to India."

In the preface of a monograph she wrote called – '*Finding the West Indies in India*' Nalini Mohabir [4] said: "Whether in Canada or India, I am always asked, 'Where do you come from?' She felt that it was s question posed only to those who do not belong. "When asked, I like to answer: 'I am from here (Kolkata/Delhi/Ajmer or wherever I find myself) because this is where I am at the present moment. I am also from Canada (where I was born) Guyana (on my father's side), Trinidad (on my mother's side). I belong to many places. The follow-up question inevitably is, 'Yes, but are you Indian? My answer? 'I am from there, but yes, I am also from here.'"

Call it a quest for identity, wrote Gauitra Bahadur, as she explained the strong pull India exerts on people of Indian origin. Gauitra was also seeking to trace her grandmother's voyage to the Caribbean and was able to visit her ancestral village in Uttar Pradesh. "It may be a postcolonial cliché, but its raw and nervy and real nevertheless. Most Indo-Caribbeans I know suffer from the phantom leg syndrome; they have felt the absence of the severed limb of India for generations," she added.

Alia Somani was troubled with questions of ethnicity and decided to explore and understand her Indian heritage. She was on a tour to India to research two events that had a deep impact on the Indo-Canadian diaspora – the bombing of the Air India aircraft in

1985 and the Komagata Maru incident when the ship carrying Indian migrants was turned away from Canada in 1914. While in India, she travelled to Rajkot, the city in Gujarat from where her grandparents migrated to Tanzania. Alia Somani learnt about ethnicity while she was in graduate school when the question of race was discussed in her class. Race and ethnicity have a contemporary significance in multi-racial Canada. The classroom discussion referred to the situation of South Asians in Canada and going into history it explained why South Asians did not feel part of Canada for a long time. Alia realised that there was a sense of 'unbelonging' that exists even now in the second generation of Indian origin migrants.

Alia's grandparents were from Rajkot, they moved to Tanzania where Alia's parents were born. Her grandfather left for Tanzania from Rajkot in 1920 and reached Mbeya town. Her mother's family lived in Dar es Salaam, both families were in business. In the 1970s the Somanis migrated to Canada and Alia's parents met in Canada and got married; Alia was born in Canada. The Somanis history of migration makes them 'two times displaced'. "I cannot forget the Tanzanian part of my heritage since it is the place where my parents were born," said Alia.

The first generation immigrants have an idea of a homeland, the place that they just left, but for the second generation there is no imagined home and the country of residence, in this case Canada is not really home. An individual can have multiple identities depending on the kind of influences he or she has undergone. Being Indian is not just language, religion, rituals and value systems, but some ancient kinship which derives from being considered Indian. This implies that even an Indian who cannot speak an Indian language, does not adhere to Indian cultural patterns or value systems, is still an Indian based on an essential Indian core.

Another young *pravasi* Indian explained that he was born in Australia, but he felt isolated in the country of his birth. When he went to the country where his parents were born he felt like a visitor, a sojourner in Fiji. His ethnicity proclaimed him to be Indian but he had no knowledge of India. "I sometimes feel that I cannot lay claim to any of these countries and ask myself where exactly do I belong. Then I tell myself I am a bit of both, for I cannot ignore my ethnicity and the cultural strands that came to me through Fiji."

For the people of Indian descent living in the former colonies the question of their Indian identity and affinity was quite different. Indians were taken as indentured labourers to work on the sugarcane plantations; their descendants now form a substantial minority in the former colonies. As the colonies became independent there was a great need to make a collective identity for the new nation and it became necessary to play down the affinity to the home country. They retained their cultural and religious traditions in the former colonies, but the internal politics of these countries made it inadvisable to emphasise any ties with India. To second and third generation overseas Indians, India became a faded picture that existed in the memories and tales of elderly relatives. Winds of change and better communications, Indian films and music helped to revive the Indian connection with younger generations of overseas Indians in recent times.

Former prime minister of Trinidad and Tobago, Basdeo Panday made a trip to Lachmanpur, the small village in the Azamgarh district of Uttar Pradesh from where his parents began their journey to Trinidad. It was a deeply emotional visit and Panday [5] wrote about it in the foreword of a book by family historian Shamshu Deen on tracing the roots of Trinidadians in India: "The visit to my ancestral village of Lachmanpur was emotionally overwhelming. Words cannot express the feeling of meeting your blood relatives whom so short a time ago you never knew existed." Panday made an oblique reference to the negative responses to any assertion of Indian identity in Trinidad. He said that a former prime minister of Trinidad had once said that there was no Mother India, no Mother Africa, and no Mother China; only Mother Trinidad and Tobago. But Panday added, "That may be so. But how can you forget grandmothers India, Africa and China?"

Basdeo Panday's visit to his ancestral village sparked off a similar urge among many other Trinidadians of Indian origin to look for the place of origin of their ancestors. In Mauritius, Indians were making efforts to locate their ancestral places in India after copies of the emigration passes of all Indian indentured workers (which gave their home addresses) were placed in the Mahatma Gandhi Institute. Indians could access the emigration passes and obtain vital information about their ancestors that helped them in their search.

The desire to locate family origins is a deeply felt need and searchers use all the means available to search for that family link. One enterprising Indian based in London managed to obtain the phone number of the police post in Jalalabad in Shahjahanur district but found that he could not communicate with the policemen. They could not understand what he wanted and he could not follow their language. He wrote a plaintive appeal to the Antar Rashtriya Sahyog Parishad, a non-governmental organisation, saying, "I have the telephone number of the police post at Jalalabad, but they do not speak English. I do not speak any Hindi – that is a problem." Asking for assistance for his family search endeavour, he promised them that he would soon learn to speak and read Hindi, signing off as Jerry Shailindra Kumar Singh.

Minal Hajratwala's[6] extended family is dispersed through five continents and she undertook meticulous research to trace the series of migrations that took the Hajratwalas around the world. Minal interviewed nearly a hundred members of her family, friends and community sources to piece together her family's story that she wrote in her book, '*Leaving India: My Family's Journey From Five Villages to Five Continents*'. Minal Hajratwala came to India "to find whatever fragments remained here, to trace the shape of our past and learn how its shadows illuminate our present."

Since written records were sparse and difficult to access, Minal began her story with a visit to the clan genealogist. In a region where people were not literate, it was the responsibility of one caste to maintain the family records of births, deaths and marriages. She reached the *pandit* in Vadodara on the strength of a name and a vague address given to her by a distant relative in Fiji. And so began her search for her family's history.

The paucity of records in the public domain and the difficulty of accessing them through government channels have made it difficult for overseas Indians to search for their antecedents. The President of Guyana and the Prime Ministers of Mauritius and Trinidad and Tobago could visit their ancestral villages in Uttar Pradesh and Bihar. But the central government in Delhi and the state governments in Lucknow and Patna had moved all the resources at their command to locate these villages and Bharrat Jagdeo, Navin Ramgoolam and Basdeo Panday could visit their ancestral homes in India. Other overseas Indians are not so fortunate. But more and more records are being digitised every day and more sources of information are becoming available.

High or low, rich or poor, all have experienced the deeply felt longing to trace their family origins. The interest in their genealogies is not confined to Indians in the old colonies, the descendants of migrants to Britain, Australia, North America and parts of Europe are also keen on learning about their antecedents and lineage. Others just want to know about the early Indians settled in Britain or the United States. There is also the increasing interest in the lives of British ancestors who had a connection with India in the colonial times. Many men and women travel to India to look for graves of their ancestors and visit the places with which they had some association.

Notes

1. *A New System of Slavery: The Export of Indian Labour Overseas, 1830-1920* by Hugh Tinker, London, Oxford University Press, 1974.
2. *Autobiography of An Indentured Labourer: Munshi Rahman Khan (1874-1972) Jeevan Prakash* translated by Kathinka Sinha-Kerkhoff, Ellen Bal and Alok Deo Singh, Shipra Publications, 2005.
3. *My twenty-one years in Fiji Islands* by Totaram Sanadhya, Fiji Museum, 1991.
4. *Finding the West Indies in India* by Nalini Mohabir.
5. *Lineages and Linkages, Solving Trinidad Roots in India*, (foreword by Basdeo Panday).
6. *Leaving India: My Family's Journey from Five Villages to Five Continents* by Minal Hajratwala, Tranquebar Press.

Starting a Genealogical Search, Ancestral Search in India

Genealogy or the pursuit of family history and lineage has become one of the most popular hobbies around the world. It used to be the preserve of professional researchers, who were occasionally asked to draw up a socially acceptable pedigree for a self-made business tycoon or a rising politician. Genealogy began to attract many more adherents when it became a personalised search as more and more government records became easily accessible to the public. It became an engrossing pastime as the internet expanded providing a great mass of easily accessible, digitised information, much of which would have been practically impossible to find some years ago.

People usually begin researching their family history to satisfy a desire to know more about their antecedents; they want to know where and how their ancestors lived and why they left the old homes to venture into a new world. Some want to know more about old family events, for others it may be a legacy or a gift of old documents and photographs from an elderly relative which may spark off an interest in a genealogical search. Others may want to get to the bottom of an old family legend or a desire to prove a connection to a famous person.

Some people begin the search to make up a medical history of the family to keep a record of diseases and medical conditions that can be inherited. Doctors are increasingly asking patients for family medical history for predisposition towards particular medical conditions. Sometimes it can be a labour of love to put together a family history book to be gifted to a favourite relative on a special occasion. A family history book can be used to give children a sense of history through who their ancestors were and the kind of lives they lived. There is even a trend of people getting their DNA tested to trace their ancestry.

It used to be the older people who took up an interest in their ancestral history but a survey done by a genealogical website showed that there was a huge increase in the number of young people doing a family history search. Drawing up family trees are among the favourite school projects for students. In South Africa, Family History is a part of the school curriculum where school children learn to draw their family tree.

Scotland planned 'Homecoming 2009' as a year of homecoming and organised a number of events, with a gathering of the clans as the centrepiece. UNESCO has supported the African Heritage Trails that commemorate the slave routes and explain the artefacts of the slave life. Birthright Israel and more recently Birthright Armenia (it is patterned on the Israeli programme) offer young members of the diaspora an intensely emotional experience of the cultural heritage of the ancestral country.

Genealogy has become a thriving business with several specialised genealogical sites becoming some of the most visited sites on the net. Family tree-maker software programmes on the internet have made family searches much more convenient. There are a large number of genealogical databases on the internet to consult; a genealogical database is a collection of information arranged in a manner that makes them easy to search to obtain specific information. Websites like Ancestry.com, which is the largest commercial genealogy site, Genealogy.com, FamilySearch.org and other internet groups have vast resources of data.

There are thousands of online genealogical databases that have a range of information, from all kinds of government records, census details, church records of baptisms, weddings and burials, shipping registers and passenger lists that can be easily accessed. Unfortunately, for an Information Technology powerhouse like India, there are only a limited number of official Indian records which are digitised and available online.

The Family History Library in Salt Lake City in Utah, USA is the largest repository of genealogical records in the world. The Library has been set up by the Church of Jesus Christ of the Latter Day Saints. Started in 1894, the records collected by the Church are stored in a massive vault built into the mountainside. The library has over 3400 branch libraries around the world that are known as Family History Centres. The Centres are open to the public for consultation and have volunteers who are willing to guide visitors on how to access the documents. Since the library adds millions of documents every year, this list keeps on growing. There is a small section that is of interest to Indians. The Genealogical Society of Utah (GSU), USA has the microfilmed *pothis* (traditional records) of Haridwar, Kurukshetra, Pehowa, Chintpurni, Jawalapur and Jawalamukhi. It is the tradition in some parts of India to maintain the family tree in a *pothi* or register with a family *panda* or priest at Hindu pilgrimage spots such as Haridwar, Benares (Varanasi), Soron etc. These *pothis* have been created over generations by the *pandas* or priests at the pilgrimage spots. The *pothis* of many pilgrimage centres have been microfilmed as part of a genealogical project.

Hindus would visit the traditional pilgrimage destination on special occasions and for immersing the ashes of cremated relatives. Each *panda* has the responsibility for pilgrims from a particular area. The panda lists down the name, home town, date and purpose of visit of each pilgrim and also makes entries on the family record of all births, weddings and deaths in the family. The information would be entered into the *pothis* or registers that are maintained by the panda and were handed down from father to son in the panda's family. However, not all Hindus have their genealogies listed with the pandas in religious places. In many areas, the family record keeper travelled through a particular region with his *pothis*, periodically visiting all the villages and adding names to the family record.

Like the revenue records, the genealogy records or the *pothis* can provide confirmation of the linkages with the family in India. A UK-based academic obtained the emigration passes of his grandparents from the National Archives in Guyana. He hired a local researcher in India to travel to the address in Agra district. By talking to town elders and shifting through the histories of the *lodh* families in the area, the research team identified one family as the relatives of the roots seeker. But the family had no recollection of anyone having left the family home and gone away.

The research team continued their search and learnt that the *lodh* community of that region went to Soron in Etah district to immerse the ashes of deceased relatives; and their genealogical records were likely to be maintained by the *pandas* of Soron. At Soron, the search team could not find the genealogical records and were directed to contact the wandering record keepers, the *jaggas* of Hindon, in the Karauli district of Rajasthan. At Hindon, the researchers met Brijesh Jagga, who showed them the record register – it was written in Mudia script so they could not read it. But Brijesh Jagga read out the family tree of Sedhu of the *lodh* caste. Sedhu's family had a Bhulle listed as one of his descendents as well as members of the family in Agra district. There was no further addition to Bhulle's line indicating that he had moved away since there was no entry for his death either. It was confirmation that the two families were related.

The Genealogical Society of Utah has the genealogical records of Maithili *brahmins* from Madhubani district in Bihar and the *kayasth* community's genealogical records. It also has the Muslim marriage records for Meerut district for the period 1881-1982, the Qazi marriage records for Bulandshahr district in Uttar Pradesh for 1921-1955. Microfilm copies of these records are also kept at the National Archives of India, New Delhi.

The GSU also has a large number of church records from India, from parish registers. The records include baptism records, marriage and burial registers and other church related information. It has Roman Catholic Church records from the territories of Goa and Pondicherry as well as some civil registration records from Pondicherry. Records of people employed in the police, railways, postal service and civil service by the British India government can be found in the Oriental and India Office collections in London.

Genealogy has not taken off in India as it has in other parts of the world. But there are a substantial number of overseas Indians interested in their ancestors' lives. There is also considerable interest in genealogical searches among British and European descendants of people who lived and worked in India during colonial times. There are several organisations and agencies that conduct special tours for tourists coming in from Britain, Europe and Australia on a tour circuit that takes them to the places associated with their ancestors. The Commonwealth War Graves Commission has lists of all the graves of British servicemen and officers buried in India. It also maintains war memorials to the men and women of the Commonwealth forces who died in the two world wars. There are also specialised tours for Anglo-Indians to visit India.

Overseas Indians like Nisha want to know the family's story of migration. Nisha began searching her family history after her friend started building up her family tree. As her friend got more engrossed in the family story of migration, she frequently talked to Nisha about her relations and ancestors in Poland and Russia and their journey to America. Hearing the migration stories, Nisha began thinking about her own family. "It made me want to seek out my own family's stories, their experiences in a small town in

Tamil Nadu where my great-grandfather was a highly respected teacher, my granduncle who went to work in Malaysia, my parents' journey to America, my cousins doing their own thing in different ways and different places. So I began a search for my own roots which had spread so far through the past hundred years. I began to feel that I was part of a legacy that had flowered in different countries that was no less fascinating than the migrations in other parts of the world. I needed to seek out my own stories of migrations," Nisha said.

The majority of overseas Indians carrying out a family search seek to locate the home of their ancestors who were taken as indentured workers to the British, French and Dutch colonies. Many of their descendants are now keen to find the old connections, and to visit the old homeland. Overseas Indians in Mauritius, Trinidad, Fiji and South Africa are keen to revive their Indian links, but it is second time migrants who went from Guyana, Trinidad, Fiji, and Suriname to the US, Canada, Britain, Europe, Australia and New Zealand who are more actively involved in searching for their roots in India.

Seeking Information

Many of the people trying to search their family roots have very little information about the place from where their grandparents and great-grandparents had migrated. Most of the information was lost over a couple of generations as many of the old timers did not want to talk about the difficult indenture days and the break with the family in India. Often they do not even know which part of India their ancestors came from or the hardship their forefathers bore when they arrived in the new land. A veil of silence was drawn over the period of *girmit*, the community wanted to put that painful period behind and move on to make a new life. By the third generation, the *girmit* times were an old story that barely registered in their consciousness – the old timers did not talk about it and nor was it part of the history books in countries like Fiji.

Searchers are sometimes not sure of their ancestors names, the ship on which they arrived or the date of arrival. Family names were anglicised in some colonies when the children of former indentured workers were admitted to church run schools or the name of the workers was changed at the plantation to which they were assigned. Often the original name was lost entirely from the family memory.

It would seem practically impossible to carry out a family search in these circumstances. But a family search is all about seeking information from different sources, following up leads and meticulously building up a family tree. Genealogists say that it is surprising the amount of information that can be gathered from within the family even when people say that they don't know anything about their parents or grandparents' history.

One key document for connecting the family to an ancestral home in India is the emigration pass. Every indentured worker was issued an emigration pass when they migrated. A copy of the emigration pass was handed over to the indentured worker, one copy was placed in the emigration records of the host country on arrival of the worker and one copy was retained in the Indian emigration records. The emigration pass was issued under the terms of the Indian Emigration Act of 1883 at the Emigration Depots for each Indian leaving the country under an indenture service contract. The emigration passes were issued by the Emigration Agent of the importing colony after the approval of the Protector of Emigrants and the Depot Surgeon certifying the emigrant to be in good health. Aside from the personal details of the emigrant with his address, each pass was stamped with the date of issue and the name and number of the ship on which the emigrant was to travel.

The emigration pass was compared with the list of emigrants on arrival at the colony. It was further stamped with the immigrant's number according to the General Register of Indian Immigrants; a number that was used for all other official documents such as end of indenture certificate etc. Each of the former colonies has the emigration records of the indentured workers. The colonial administrators were meticulous record keepers but with the passage of time and poor maintenance some of the old records have decayed and got lost.

The best maintained and easily accessible indenture migration records are the Suriname records. The information on the emigration passes of indentured workers in Suriname is online – a mere click on a computer key will bring the information on the screen together with the software to translate the Dutch language into English. Parmanand Singh searching for his ancestor, Punno Singh was pleasantly surprised at the ease with which he could access the information that he was looking for. The trail was less easy to follow when his ancestor moved from Suriname to Guyana.

The Suriname emigration certificate gives the following information – given name, gender, age, skin colour, height, distinguishing features, nationality, district of origin, police station, village name, profession, caste/religion, children, ship's name, sign-up number, recruitment agency, place of departure, date of departure, place of arrival, plantation, planter, immigration register, contract starts, contract ends, renewal of contract and resistance activities.

The website of the National Archives at The Hague has the Suriname Census of 1921. The Census report lists the names of everyone who lived in Suriname in the year 1921. It gives the name of all family members living in the same household. The Archives has the birth records of the district of Paramaribo, the capital of Suriname, for the period 1828-1906 and also some records of marriages and deaths of that period, though not all of them.

The Ships Register also list emigration details certifying the immigrant's fitness to work, name of the ship and the date of its arrival, name of the immigrant, his caste and his father's name, the immigrant's sex, age, next of kin, village and district address in India, occupation, whether married and the name of their spouse and children. The emigration passes for Trinidad, Mauritius, Fiji, Guyana and South Africa have similar information. This valuable document gives the address of the ancestral home in India for a searcher to get started on his quest in India. In some cases the emigration pass also gives the name of the next of kin, usually father or brother, which helps to identify relatives in the ancestral homeland.

Emigration passes for arrivals in Mauritius are kept at the Mahatma Gandhi Institute and are easily accessible. The National Archives of Fiji has a complete set of emigration passes of over 60,000 emigration passes placed in 240 large folios and copies are listed according to year and ship of arrival as well as in alphabetical order. The passes are also available on microfilm that is accessible at the National Archives.

The National Archives in Guyana are in good shape now and the staff and archivists are quite willing to help those who come in search of information. But those records that got destroyed during the long period of neglect are lost to researchers; the emigration passes for the years 1838 to 1865 are missing. For those whose ancestors emigration passes cannot be found, there are other documents that may help provide clues and bits of information. The estate records of some of the large plantations are stored at the archives; the estate registers have the details of the indentured workers – the year and ship of arrival, and other information including when the period of indenture came to an end.

In South Africa, the Durban Archives Repository has the Indian shipping lists that contain the list of passengers on each ship prepared by the ship's captain. The bound volumes of the shipping lists were kept with the Department of Indian Affairs and were microfilmed and later computerised as part of a history project of the University of Durban-Westville. The passenger list has the name of the indentured worker, his place of origin and a colonial number that was given at the time of departure from India. This colonial number remained with the migrant through his life; on his marriage certificate, on the birth certificates of his children, any official documents and employment agreements and on his death certificate.

In case the emigration pass or the estate register is not available, there is another route for tracing ancestors. The archives are also the repository for the old birth and death records. The old death registers entered the name of the former indentured worker, his date of arrival aside from other details. The birth registers carried the names of the parents and in case of former indentured workers, they also mentioned the ship on which they arrived and the date of arrival. Trace the trail through the birth records of your parents, their parents and the ancestor who came from India.

The National Archives of Trinidad and Tobago has the immigration details of Indian migrants who arrived in the colony between 1845 and 1917. There are however, some gaps in the registers for this period. The Archives has the emigration passes of 120,000 migrants out of the total 147,597 indentured workers who arrived in Trinidad. There are other documents available under the category, General Registers for the years 1845-1917, Ship Registers from 1866-1917 and some Estate Registers for the period 1845-1901 that can be consulted to obtain information on the indentured workers.

The archives also have records of those migrant workers who returned home to India. A significant number of indentured workers returned to India and some of them re-indentured themselves to either the same country or to another colony depending on the ship that was ready to sail. The worker had 'Returnee of Mauritius' or Trinidad or St Vincent as the case may be written against their name in the General Register and the Shipping Register.

Not all Indian migrants to the colonies went as indentured labourers; many came in as 'free' migrants. As fare paying passengers on the ships, they did not have an emigration pass. Sometimes, Indians completed their indenture period and moved on to some other colony – Punno Singh went to Suriname as an indentured worker and then went to Guyana with his family. A few thousand Indians went to Suriname from Guyana, while others moved to the smaller Windward Islands like Martinique, St Lucia and St Vincent as well as Guadeloupe in the Leeward Islands. Voluntary migrants were usually not cut off from their relatives in India like the indentured workers. They were likely to have remained in touch with the family back home for some time.

There are a few fortunate families who have a copy of the emigration pass of their ancestor in their possession. But most people have only some vague knowledge of where their ancestor came from. That is, however, not the end of the road for most overseas Indians can apply to the National Archives and ask for a copy of the emigration pass. But to apply for a copy of the emigration certificate, it is necessary to have the correct name of the indentured worker, year of arrival, and name of the ship to be able to locate the record.

A large number of people wanting to start a search find that they do not have this crucial information. It is quite likely that this information may be available in bits and pieces with different members of the extended family. Searchers have to hunt for these bits of information and put them together to carry on with their roots exploration.

There are many web groups on the net that seek to help ancestral searchers. Several of them are oriented towards descendants of indentured workers from the Pacific or the Caribbean region. The interactive sites allow members to post their search experiences and also ask questions which are answered by other members of the group. They often relate personal experiences and offer suggestions or solutions to problems. Group members' post queries, seek information, search and exchange data about their family history, genealogy and learn about the indenture experience that their ancestors went through.

Posting a message on a message board can get a response from someone who can help you. Atma Ramchalaon was trying to locate two villages in Uttar Pradesh where his grandparents were born. He posted a query on a message board on the net. Some days later he got a response to his mail from a person who recognised the names of the villages and could give Ramchalaon directions on how to reach those villages. But, not all seekers are so lucky!

Starting a Search

So, you want to start a family search – there are some things you have to do right away. The very first thing you should do is to get together all old documents and personal papers that you can find. These include birth and death certificates of your parents and grandparents, school leaving certificates, property documents, wills, bank papers etc. These old papers can often give a name of a place or a person that you are looking for and also provide valuable clues that can open up more productive avenues for the search.

After collecting the old documents, make copies of all of them. There is an amazing tendency for old and personally valuable documents to get lost, damaged or misplaced. It is important to remember that photostat copies of documents can fade away. It is best to either scan or make at least two sets of copies of the more important documents.

The most important source of information for a search are members of your own family, especially the elderly relatives; the gossipy old aunts, the uncle who loves talking about the days gone by, the cousin who keeps tabs on all the relatives. Indians do not usually write diaries or memoirs, the family history is carried forward by the pundits or the older women in the family. In fact, it helps to talk to all your elderly relatives and family friends – any one of them could remember the elusive date or name or ship's name that you have been chasing for months.

They are a fund of anecdotes and stories that bring to life people who are just a name till then. Even those who have a grievance and have hoarded all the hurts of the past, have things to tell that can give a valuable clue. Talk to the oldest relations first; and try and tape record the conversations whenever possible. As one leading genealogist said, "if only" are the saddest words for a searcher, who has missed the opportunity to speak to an aged relative.

Make a list of the names and addresses of all your older relatives and family connections. Get in touch with each one of them individually and tell them that you are planning to start on a family search. Set up appointments to meet with them. Ask them, in the meantime, to look through the old documents they have for anything that might help you in your search. People have a surprising amount of stuff tucked away in odd corners of the house; offer to help sort out old papers, you may come across something significant. Old newspaper clippings, obituary notices, insurance documents, school leaving certificates can provide that crucial date or name.

If it is not possible to meet older relatives personally, it is a good idea to speak to them on the phone or write them a letter telling them about your plans and asking for their help. Ask them specific questions so that they can begin trying to recall facts and events. Ask any relative or friend who lives close by to go and visit the relatives and listen to their responses to the questions. Often memories return gradually and sometimes they get lost again.

Some of the family stories have faded away with just a few remaining fragments. Andy Sheoram found a cornucopia of stories when he prodded a couple of his grandaunts to talk about the old days at a family reunion in Trinidad. Andy's elderly aunt recalled her mother saying that Sheoran had left home after a fight. Andy's great-grandfather, Sheoram ran away from home after a disagreement with his uncle (*chacha*). Sheoram and his uncle were working in the fields on a hot day when his uncle asked him to run an errand. Sheoram refused to run home to fetch some sherbet in the heat and his uncle had thrown a clod of earth at him. Sheoram left home that afternoon; he later met some recruiters and signed up to go to Trinidad.

In every family there is usually one person who remembers old events, dates, which cousin is older than the other, how distant relations are connected to the family and such like. That person is likely to be the most informative about family history. After speaking to your immediate family members, seek out that family historian for getting the most information.

Ask a lot of questions of your elderly kin, and go back to them again if you can to ask more questions after talking to other relatives. Usually it is the older female relatives who prove to be a fount of information about the family; the achievements, the foibles and the scandals. Also try and meet close family friends who are considered part of the extended family or *jahajis* – they can have a fund of stories and information about your parents and grandparents, especially if they had kept in close touch with each other.

Sheila's great-grandmother arrived in Trinidad accompanied by her 12-year-old son, but Sheila did not know the name of the ship or the year they arrived. She spent many months asking her relatives if they knew the name of the ship which brought their ancestors. During a visit back home to Trinidad, Sheila met members of the extended family and asked the same questions without much success. Then at the wedding of a second cousin, she met a middle-aged couple; Sheila faintly recalled that her grandmother was very fond of these 'relatives'.

It was while talking to the old lady that Sheila learnt why that family had special kinship ties with her family. The lady's father had travelled on the same ship as Sheila's great-grandmother and grandfather! The lady did not know the year they reached Trinidad but she remembered her grandmother mentioning the name of a ship. That was an important clue that set Sheila on the path of locating her ancestor's emigration pass.

There are a few things to keep in mind when conducting an oral history interview. When meeting an elderly relative, make it a social event rather than go armed with a questionnaire. Let it be a story telling, reminiscing occasion. Let them talk at their own pace, just gently edging them back to the main story if they tend to wander. Though it is best to record the interview, some people can get intimidated by a tape recorder, so be ready to take notes. Try and get a small machine and place it unobtrusively on the side. Everyone loves to be photographed, so take a few pictures to put them at ease. Take notes if you have to, but show that you are interested in what is being said – nod and smile.

Ask a short but relevant question that takes the story forward. But don't let the question interrupt the flow of thought – let them complete the anecdote or you might break the thought process. Trinidadian genealogist, Shamshu Deen said that he has been able to get crucial information from elderly people, even those suffering from Alzheimer's. He explained that people with Dementia or Alzheimer's have lost their short term memory but they still retain their long term memory. They can often recall events that took place a long time ago – just put them at ease and let them talk.

Some people are reluctant to talk about themselves; they are likely to say that there was nothing of interest in their life stories. It may take a bit of time and effort to get them to open up. One of the best ways to start is to talk to them about a well remembered event; how and why it happened and what their feelings were at that time. It can slowly open the floodgates of reminiscences. Every person's version is different; they may give a more graphic description about the same event and add to the main story. Some of their stories can trigger off the memory of another relative.

Everyone has their own version of stories and people, especially older people do not like to be questioned on their version. If you have old photographs, take them along, it is surprising how pictures bring back old memories and feelings. Ask to see the relatives own photo albums – people love to show their pictures and talk about them.

An interview may not be a one off thing, if possible go back after some time for another chat. Family gatherings on festive occasions, weddings and funerals are a good time to get a few relatives talking about the old days. They jog each other's memories and embellish the stories with their own thoughts and feelings. Photographs can give clues about people and it is surprising which clue can lead one to a big discovery.

Cliff Pereira's family had originally come from Goa; they had lived in East Africa and then moved to Europe. Pereira had been looking for family connections when he found a photograph of his great-grandfather in a naval uniform. He enlarged the photograph and took it to an expert on medals. The expert identified three of the medals as World War 1 medals. Pereira contacted the British Ministry of Defence and obtained some information about the Navy. Later, Pereira found a list of Goans in the British Royal Navy and learnt of his great-grandfather's military history.

It is most important to keep a record of all the information you gather. Makes copies of all documents and write down the source and date of every bit of information. As your search progresses, bits of information that did not seem significant at that time may suddenly acquire great importance at a later stage. And it is most frustrating to try and rack one's brains trying to recall who gave you that piece of information. Trained genealogists say that even the best researcher can overlook something important in a document and may need to go back and take another look at it, especially if fresh evidence is available.

Keep a log of the websites you have visited, the date and the result of the search for future reference. One may need to go back to relook a particular piece of evidence; and it is a tedious process to wade through a number of websites to find the site with the information one is looking for. It is also advisable to look for spelling variations – names of places have changed over the years, such as Kolkata for Calcutta, Chennai for Madras. Also different spellings were used for the same name.

If you are planning to make a trip to look through government records, find out the timings of the record office or archives and also if the documents you are seeking are at that office. Make a phone call or email to check if the material you need is available or not. Also go through the catalogue if it is available online, it will save a great deal of time when you go to the Archives. I remember going to the National Archives in Suva, Fiji to look for old documents relating to my grandfather and finding that it was early closing at the Archives that day because of a parade. Fortunately, I had the relevant dates and file numbers that helped the clerk to locate the files I wanted. I managed to get copies of the documents just as the office closed for the day.

Family history is not just a set of names and dates on a family tree or even a series of events; it needs the small details and personal memories to bring the story alive. It is family folklore of reminiscences – the hunting trip that resulted in the awkwardly shaped book-ends that have been handed down one generation of the family to the other. It is the answers to questions like 'why did dad's elder brother leave Rangoon and go to Natal', or 'why did cousin, Shiv buy a Studebaker when he could not drive?' – that go to make the story interesting. There are also stories that were too painful to talk about when memories were fresh and now have slowly faded from the family memory – such as the sudden departure from Kenya to Canada in the 1970s after grandfather lost the grocery business to the process of Africanisation.

Oral history is important not just to get information that would help to trace ancestral history. Oral history is living history, stories told by people who were present or who heard them from older relatives. They are the family stories that are handed down through the generations, from grandparents to grandchildren. They give a sense of the family history at a personal level. They tell the younger generation of events that took place in the past. A family tree usually gives a series of bare facts and dates; of dates of birth, marriage, emigration and death and the number of children.

Sometimes we want to know more about the names on the family tree; to know the larger picture of how they led their lives and the changes that have taken place. Many people don't just try to make a family tree or find out where their ancestors migrated from in India. They try to get a feel of their ancestors' life, the conditions they lived in and their reasons for migrating.

Join a mailing list in order to connect with other people who are on a similar search. Messages sent to the list are circulated to the entire membership of the mailing list. They can be a source of inspiration, advice and assistance. There are websites and chat sites for people of Indian origin whose ancestors came from India to Trinidad, Guyana, Suriname or Fiji. They are usually able to get tips on how to go about obtaining information and how to access documents that can give them information about their ancestors. Indo-Caribbeans from the smaller Caribbean islands usually try to contact other Caribbean island groups for information and advice.

Karen from Australia wrote on a website: "I'm looking for information on Bingingee Sorobjee Pochee (several different spellings) Born 1833 Bombay and arriving in Australia sometime before 1861. He was a photographer in Military Square Lane in Bombay and believed to have been married and widowed and having at least a daughter although he didn't bring her to Australia.

He remarried in Parramatta, NSW in 1861 and had a son in 1863 named Sorabjee Bingingee Pochee in Ipswich QLD. His wife, Mary Ann died in 1902, he left Parramatta sometime after 1904 and disappeared. Rumours suggest he may have gone back to India to die. He was a Parsee Indian and believed to have been at one time, the royal court's photographer. Can anyone help me find his death record?" Five people responded to her mail with suggestions.

It is worthwhile making a visit to the national archives with all bits of available information. It can, sometimes be possible to locate vital clues that lead to a reference to the ancestor in the records. Praveen Chandra and Saras Chandra wrote about their hunt for their great grandfather's story in '*Bittersweet: Voices from the Past*',[1] that was published to mark the 125th anniversary of the Indian arrival in Fiji. All that Chandra knew about his great grandfather, Baijnath was that he came to Fiji as an indentured worker and that he was convicted and hanged for a murder he may not have committed. He knew neither the year of arrival nor the ship his grandfather travelled on.

The Fiji National Archives used to list the emigration passes on the basis of year of arrival, but had later added lists of arrivals in alphabetical order as well. At the Archives, Chandra made a request for the 'B' register and found 44 Baijnaths in the record book. He asked to see the emigration passes for all the Baijnaths. It was a daunting task but Chandra was able to shorten the list by removing all those who had arrived after 1900. Chandra's father (Baijnath's grandson) was born in 1919 so arrivals after that date (1900) could safely be eliminated. It left him with four names but with no way to prune them further.

Dr Kamlesh Sharma was also in a similar position of not having many details about his great-grandfather and his uncle's arrival in Fiji when he began his search at the National Archives. Sharma knew that his grandfather had served his *girmit* in Ba area. While looking through the register with his name, he found that out of the five similar names in the register, only one had been allocated to Ba, so he could identify his grandfather's emigration pass. For his *mausa* (uncle) it was an easier search since he was the only one of that name in the register. But in the case of his great-grandmother, there were too many similar names in the register and he had to give up the search.

Fortunately for Chandra, he met former politician and historian Dr Ahmed Ali, who was doing his own research at the Archives. Dr Ali pointed him in a different direction; he suggested that Chandra look through the death registers instead of the arrival registers since the death registers would list the cause of death. Chandra waded through the registers till he came upon Baijnath, cause of death – judicial hanging – hanged at Suva Jail – 17 March, 1913. The next three entries had the same comment in the last column for Ramkumar Singh, Kallu and Houba.

The death register also had a file reference number, 1720/1913 and Dr Ali said that would be the reference number for the court files of the case. Chandra looked up the old newspaper files for March 1913 when the local newspaper would have reported the hanging of the four men. The case file took some time to be located but it contained details of the case. The file had the names, statements, a sketch of the crime scene, three death warrants and a petition signed by a number of villagers requesting a pardon for the accused men.

Chandra was elated to see a submission made to the Governor of Fiji by one of the defence lawyers, Reginald Berkeley, in which the lawyer claimed that the guilty verdict was reached on circumstantial and fabricated evidence from unreliable witnesses. The file confirmed the family view of the sad event. According to family history a great injustice had been done to Baijnath; that the culprit was a well known trouble-maker who lived in the same village of Vitogo in Lautoka.

In 2003, the Chandras went to India to Baijnath's village of Bhatwari Kalan. They could not find any relatives in Bhatwari

Kalan, but it was an emotional moment. Chandra wrote about his visit: "I felt that some part of Baijnath had returned to the motherland. It was like a homecoming."

Once you have the emigration pass and the address of the village, there is still the business of locating the place in India. For searchers living far away from India, it is not easy to find the village on a map. That is a different kind of search.

Ancestral Search in India

Family history searches in India require different set of resources as there are very few trained genealogists in India. At the same time, official records are difficult to access and few of them are available on the internet. But intrepid ancestral searchers, armed with a village name, father's name and next of kin, have used a variety of methods to discover their family history.

Locating a remote village deep in the heart of rural India is not an easy job as there can be several villages with similar sounding names. Sometimes the names on the emigration passes were mis-spelled or written phonetically, adding to the difficulty in identifying the village. Names of the districts have changed and to further complicate matter, the tehsils and blocks of villages have moved to different districts when the districts were re-organised. Some villages have disappeared altogether- swept away by floods. Small hamlets have been abandoned after a raging disease killed a number of the inhabitants, and others have merged into the expanding small towns in the neighbourhood.

Most searchers have relied on genealogists, researchers, private detectives, not-for-profit social organisations, and government search programmes to locate the villages. A few have taken help from friends and acquaintances and even ventured out themselves accompanied by a local guide.

Chat sites and newsletters on the internet are another fount of information and help. Photojournalist, Atman Ramchalaon used various interactive web groups to get help and directions on how to start a genealogical search. He began his search on the request of his 85-year-old mother in Mauritius; she had told him that it was her last wish to learn about her roots before she died. Ramcharon's great-grandmother, Luchminia Cokil was born in Aamghat village in Ballia district in UP and had migrated to Mauritius in 1896. A stranger on a webchat site responded to Ramchalaon's appeal, saying that he knew the villages mentioned in the web post. It helped Ramchalaon get a general sense of the location of Aamghat village in Garouli tehsil. But locating his grandfather, Kunjbihari Ramchalaon's village was not so easy.

Atman took the assistance of the Antar Rashtriya Sahyog Parishad for the search. Kunjbihari Ramchalaon arrived in Mauritius as a 20-year-old on 18 Sept 1871. He was employed by a company called Summerville in the district of Riviere du Ramparts working as a stable hand. He was good with horses and after completing his indenture contract, he started a livery stable business. Horses were the main mode of transportation and Kunjbihari made a good living. In 1892 he decided to visit his parents in India. While in India he got married to Luchminia of Aamghat village. Sometime later, Kunjbihari and Luchminia and two servants, Lauthur Ganguly and Mohan Boram sailed on SS Akbar from Bombay to Mauritius.

Kunjbihari's village was listed as Skaria, Rasra police station in Ghazipur district. Rasra is now part of Ballia which was taken out from Ghazipur district and made into a separate district. But there were several villages named Sikaria in Ballia district – Sikaria kala, Sikaria kalan, Sikaria khund in Rasra block, Sikaria in Chilkara block, and Sikaria on Belthara Road. There was also a Sikaria in Ratanpura block and Sikaria in Haldhapur, situated on the border of Ballia and Mau district. Rasra tehsil had been part of Ghazipur district till Ballia was carved out of it; later Mau district was formed with parts of Ballia and Azamgarh district. All the other Sikarias had to be painstakingly eliminated to locate Kunjbihari's village.

Atman was able to visit the village and trace some relatives, and capture the moment on film. Unfortunately, he could not locate the home village of his maternal great-grandfather. He fell sick while searching for Tarrowa village in Chapra district and decided to return home. But Chapra remains on his list of future destinations!

The methodology used to trace villages in India have been similar – get a general location of the nearest small town and if possible of the tehsil or block where the village lies. Hire local researchers to go through the official records. Find the location of the police station mentioned in the ancestor's address, go to the police station and get directions to the ancestral village. Stop along the way to talk to friendly villagers to get more precise directions and ask about other settlements of the caste group one is searching for.

Nalini Mohabir[2] carried out field research work in India to locate the people who had returned to India from the Caribbean in 1955; she had to trace their journey back to their villages. Nalini was also on a personal quest – to locate the links to her own great-grandparents. As a young girl, Nalini had heard stories about Guyana and her family's migration to Canada. But it in was in 2006 when she was studying for her masters degree in Immigration and Settlement Studies that she began a series of long conversations with her grandfather, Chhablal Ramcharan. From her *aja*, Nalini learnt of her own family's history of migration and the story of the *girimityas* last return journey to India. The indentured workers had the right to return to India after they completed their period of indenture. It is estimated that about 30 per cent of the indentured workers returned to India. The MV Resurgent was the last repatriation ship that brought back the final group of returning indentured workers from the Caribbean to India in 1955. Nalini's *aja*, Chhablal Ramcharan was the Repatriation Officer, who accompanied the returning *girmitiyas* to India. Nalini was intrigued by the indentured workers wanting to return to India at such a late stage and she planned to follow the journey of the MV Resurgent and its passengers to their homes in India.

As Nalini planned her academic quest, she also obtained the emigration passes of three of her great-grandparents from the National Archives in Guyana. When she was packing her bags to fly to India, Nalini's father asked her to visit their ancestral village and bring back a bottle full of soil from the village that was somewhere in Faizabad district. Her father's simple request showed her the depth of sentiment and emotion that were tied up to her search.

Nalini's personal odyssey took her to Ajmer but she could not find any links to her great-grandmother, Kariman. She was however luckier with her great-grandfather's village – Dewarya. Her great-grandfather, Ramcharan, son of Sheoraj, left Faizabad's Dewarya village in 1896. Nalini was fortunate to find a contact, who was well versed in local lore. He told her that Dewarya village was now part of Barunbazar. But a tour of Barunbazar did not provide any clues till one man said that there was a locality called Ranibazar where many people of the Kalwar caste had settled. Kalwar was the caste stated on the emigration pass, though the community now used Jaiswal as their caste name.

At Ranibazar, Nalini came across some men from the Kalwar community who took her to meet a young man called Vipin Jaiswal. His 95-year-old grandmother, Bagdai, was still alive, they said. Bagdai's memory was fading but she gave the names of her parents-in-law as Shivraj and Latchmi. Shivraj or Sheoraj was the name of Ramcharan's father. Bagdai also recalled that that her husband, Dukhi had an older brother, Ramcharan who had gone away. Dukhi had two sons, Om Prakash, Vipin's father and Ganga Prasad who lived in Mumbai. Bagdai's old memories had confirmed that this was the family Nalini was looking for. Nalini had found the old connections.

The right to return was part of the indenture contract and pressure had built up on the Guyanese government to make arrangements for the return of former indentured workers. The Guyanese government tried to dissuade them and the Indian government also tried to explain that the former indentured workers would find it difficult to adjust in the villages back in India. But the former *girmitiyas* were adamant on exercising their right to return. The majority of the returnees were moved by the nostalgic pull of the motherland. As they grew older the yearning to have their ashes immersed in the Ganga had grown stronger.

Eminent Caribbean author, David Dabydeen wrote about the voyage of the MV Resurgent in an introduction to the book, '*The First Crossing*', [3] the edited version of the diary of Theophilus Richmond, the surgeon on board the ship, Hesperus. The Hesperus was the first ship to carry indentured workers from Calcutta to Georgetown, Guyana in 1838. The majority of the repatriates on the MV Resurgent became destitute after reaching India, according to Dabydeen. Frantic appeals were made to locate relatives in Guyana and ask them for passage money for returning to Guyana. Only a handful of the repatriates managed to get back to Guyana. It is a poignant story of repeated displacement, he wrote. The journey had a sad end for the majority of the passengers who found that India in 1955 was not like the imagined homeland that they had left so many years ago.

Mohabir recalled, "I remember my *aja* telling me that even before the Resurgent was refuelled and readied for its return journey, there was a large group of returnees gathered at the dock, clamouring to be taken on board to return to Guyana." Through painstaking research Nalini Mohabir was able to locate two returnees who were teenagers when they reached Calcutta. Dundee was born in Guyana, but his parents who hailed from Andhra Pradesh decided to return to India for sentimental reasons, spurred on by a family disagreement. Dundee's parents went to their village near Visakhapatnam, but their land had been taken over by relatives. The family moved to Chennai and Dundee, who could speak good English managed to find a job.

Chinna Gounder (now GC Naresh) was 12 years old when his extended family returned to India because of his grandparents longing for home after 40 years in Guyana. The family sold off its land and cattle and booked passage on the MV Resurgent. Arriving in India they realized it was a mistake and about a year later his grandparents and some of his uncles returned to Guyana. His elder brother, Permaloo saved some money and traveled back to Guyana on a cargo boat, but Naresh went to their native village, Padavedu in Tamil Nadu. According to Nalini, Naresh still has a slight Guyanese accent. Both Dundee and Naresh had held on to their memories of Guyana. They had gone through difficult times finding a place for themselves in the ancestral homeland.

Dr Kamlesh Sharma,[4] an Australia based solicitor, was born in Nadi, Fiji Islands. He began a search for his ancestors in India. The first task was to obtain the emigration passes. Every bit of information assists in the huge jigsaw puzzle that needs to be put together to solve the problems at hand and to reach the desired goal, according to Dr Sharma. The Fiji National Archives has registers that bear the immigration passes of the indentured workers in alphabetic order. "Seeing the register with my great-grandfather's name and emigration pass was an overwhelming experience in itself!" exclaimed Dr Kamlesh Sharma.

Drawing from his own experience of researching for his ancestral history and making a trip to India to visit his ancestors' native villages, Sharma gave some sound advice to new searchers on his website. Sharma said: "Get to know the area and its surroundings and put it in the overall context of India as a country. I recommend access to a good atlas of India (which is available in all bookshops) so that you can visualise the area from various aspects by looking at the map of India, then moving down to the state such as Uttar Pradesh and then the local district levels such as Faizabad. There is heaps of information on the Internet regarding the districts. Some examples are the Basti District that has a website with crucial information at http://basti.nic.in while Faizabad district has its website at http://faizabad.nic.in

"You can Google the name of the *thana* to get some vital information, such as where exactly it is located and who the officer in-charge is including some telephone contacts. Now, do not place too much reliance on the *thana* as the villages in India have been redistributed several times among various *thanas* in the district. However, it is good to know the original name. The village is the most crucial piece of information and the most difficult to verify remotely. The best advice at this stage would be to get its spelling right. Some of the hand writing of the British filling in the immigration pass is not very clear so care must be taken to get the correct spelling.

"Once you are able to firm the name of the village, try Google search to see if you can discover some information on the village. I tried this for my *Nani's* village and after a lengthy search, I came across some recent newspaper articles in India that mentioned the village and the district. This gave me some reassurance that the village actually existed. Getting the wrong village name can be painful down the track as you will end up in the wrong village as has happened to me in the district of Basti. This led to losing crucial time in getting to the right village, resulting in less time being available to spend in the correct village and with the new found relatives," Kamlesh Sharma advised.

Sharma went through the frustration of trying to identify the ancestral villages; he made some progress only when he got in touch with a contact in Benares Hindu University who was well versed with villages in Uttar Pradesh. He was able to confirm the existence of the village but could not locate any relatives. Sharma was fortunate to get in touch with a travel agent through the Bhojpuri network who got interested in the search. The travel agent not only helped make Sharma's tour plans but also used his resources for locating the remote villages.

Kamlesh Sharma, however misread the village name as Deradeha in Basti under the Kalwari thana. When he reached Deradeha village he could not make any connections in Deradeha village. It seemed to be a dead end but luckily for him, the policeman who was escorting Sharma recognized the name as it was written in the copy of the emigration pass – it was 'Devadeha', a village not very far from Deradeha. Sharma was able to reach Devadeha but had lost valuable time for he had to return to town by nightfall.

In 1996, genealogist Shamshu Deen came to India on a project funded by the Indian Council of Cultural Relations (ICCR) to find the present day relatives of indentured workers of Trinidad and to develop a methodology for the ancestor search. He took up 20 sample families spread across Bihar, Uttar Pradesh and Haryana; about 80 per cent of the indentured workers came from the two states of Bihar and Uttar Pradesh. Deen's search began with the emigration pass, with the ancestor's name and next of kin in India. Since the name of the person who migrated would have been forgotten by the villagers, the father's name and the next of kin became the critical connecting points.

Among the families that Shamshu Deen was searching for was the grandparents of Basdeo Panday and Deen's own great-great-grandparents, Bholate and Josemeah, his maternal grandfather's grandparents (*Nana's nana*). Both searches were successful, though there were other searches which did not yield verifiable results. Shamshu Deen advised family history seekers in his book, '*Lineages and Linkages, Solving Trinidad Roots in India*',[5] that apart from the emigration pass, other bits of information should be obtained before embarking on the search in India. Get as many details about the family and life in India – the names of as many relatives of the ancestor – brothers, sisters, uncles, nephews and even in-laws that remain in the memory of the family. The more names the better; and hopefully one of the names would be remembered in the ancestral village and would have descendents living in the village.

Nalini Mohabir wrote about the methodology she used for her research in India. She wrote: "I soon discovered that history in India has a different form and shape. It is not a paper trail history; it is a living history passed down from generation to generation." Nalini Mohabir used the ship's manifest as the document of record for the migrant. Reaching the district or small town, Nalini would visit the Sub-Divisional Magistrate or the Superintendent of Police of the district to verify village names. In case, Nalini's local contact or guide recognised the name of the village or the *thana* (police station) it was not necessary to meet the government officials.

Once she reached the village, she would meet the village *pradhan*, *sarpanch* or *mukhiya* (village headman) and show him the names on her list. He would ask members of the same caste group or religious community. Nalini said that she found caste networks most useful. She also tapped the memories of elderly men who would point her in the right direction. Other options were going through the land records kept with the patwari or the land revenue records at the *tehsil* revenue office. According to Nalini Mohabir, "each individual's understanding of family stories and background affects their ethnic consciousness, just because we may move and move again, we do not lose our sense of place."

About the first step to take while planning a family search in India is to obtain a map of India, a map of the state to which the ancestor belonged such as Bihar or Uttar Pradesh or Tamil Nadu in order to become familiar with the region. A map of the district would be an added help as it would list the larger villages and the police stations. Indian districts are quite large and sometimes it may be easier to approach a particular village from the adjoining district than from its own district headquarters. Studying a state map would give a general idea of the area and make it easier to pin point the well known landmarks. A visit to the District Magistrate, the official in charge of the district can be most useful in getting information and assistance.

Other officials like the sub-divisional magistrates, block development officers and the police chiefs of the district could also render valuable assistance. The district or block officials can provide information on the villages. Police stations usually have a list of the villages under their jurisdiction pasted on the wall of the *thana*. An official letter of introduction about the search from the home government or the Indian High Commission or the High Commissioner of the home country in Delhi is usually an aid in explaining the quest and getting quick and courteous attention. While talking to the District Magistrate, it is a good idea to get permission to visit the Record Centre. Record room officials are not usually helpful in locating old files but the permission from the District Magistrate should make a difference in their attitude.

At the Record Centre, hire someone to search the records of the period around the time of departure of the ancestor; the records will be written in archaic Persian, old Hindi or *Kaithi*. Look for the names of the ancestor, his father and the person who inherited the lands. The death register, the family registers – *parivar* (family) and voters lists (if available) are other sources of information. The village *patwari* records the ownership of village land and the name of the person who is actually tilling the land.

While there may be people who remember someone who had left the village and gone far away, the most authentic evidence regarding an ancestor comes from the land records. However, the land records only list the owner of the land or the person cultivating the land. In case the ancestor belonged to an artisan community or did not own any agricultural land in the village it would be difficult to verify the claim through land records. In that case, it is the oral history of the village that can provide the evidence.

There are times when Indian villagers have moved to another village, either because of some dispute, or loss of land or to stay with relatives. Harish Boodhoo's relatives had moved out of the old ancestral village, the search team was directed to another village where they had shifted and then found the relatives in a third village where they had settled in Hazirabagh district.

On reaching a village, seek out the *sarpanch* – the elected village head, village elders (with long memories) and people from the ancestor's caste. Indian villages usually have one dominant caste with a mix of other castes performing different occupations. Villagers in India generally used only one name, the practice of using a surname came into vogue in the 20th century. There can be more than one person with the same name in the village, so it becomes easier to identify people through their castes. Village or family folk songs can be another indicator, since there is some amount of improvisation in the songs sung on special occasions. Often the songs refer to significant events that have taken place in the village or the family, such as a member of the family going away to foreign lands.

The methodology used by the non-governmental organization – Sri Ramanand Sarawati Pustakalya (SRSP) search team was to begin with asking the oldest person in the group his name, his father's name, grand-father's name. Ask if anyone had left the village, went far away (*door desh gayae*) and never returned. Hopefully, one of the names on the list will come up in the answers to the questions. Do not mention the ancestor's name or next of kin in the initial conversation. It was best not to mention all names and relationships at the outset. "The main idea was not to put words in people's mouths," according to Nagendra, the SRSP researcher. It is best to look for the ancestor's relative who remained in India – either the father or the brother. For it is more likely that the person who stayed on in the village would be remembered by his friends and descendents. After locating one name, ask about the other names and their relationship with the first name as a means of verification.

Searching for one's roots and eventually meeting distant relatives can sometimes be fraught with underlying tension. Yogesh Prasad, a resident of Vancouver, was among the first successful searches carried out by the UP tourism department. Yogesh Prasad's great-grandfather had gone to Fiji in 1905 as an indentured labourer and the family had lost all contact with their kin in a remote village in Gorakhpur district of UP.

For an emotional Prasad, who always longed to know about his place of origin and accidentally stumbled on the UP tourism site while surfing on the net, it was "a dream come true". He was able to visit Dangipar, where he found his kin, including a great-aunt. But Yogesh Prasad had a few apprehensions about the search to start with, apprehensions that are shared by many on a similar ancestral search. "We were initially guarded as we realized that there would be no dearth of wannabe relatives for a person settled abroad," Prasad explained. "But the state tourism department had done all the home work and our inquiries at the village confirmed that it was our village. I was very excited at visiting my native place." Yogesh Prasad's search had a happy ending, but there are instances when nagging doubts remain especially when there is no corroborative evidence about the authenticity of the relatives.

Most roots seekers who are fortunate to find distant cousins usually have a joyous reunion of the two sides of the family. Occasionally, some overseas Indians who have reached unannounced at an ancestral village have been dismayed at the cool reception they receive from their relatives. The relatives are reluctant to acknowledge the visitors as their kin. This can happen due to misunderstanding of the motives of the visitor. Researchers have been treated with suspicion and on one occasion it was a letter of introduction written by a high government functionary that helped to sort out the misunderstanding. In another instance, the new arrivals were mistaken for revenue assessors. Indian villagers are inherently suspicious of government employees and getting embroiled in official business to their detriment.

In the case of Harish Boodhoo, the ARSP team and Harish Boodhoo were surprised at the response from the relatives. The relatives believed that Boodhoo had come to claim his grandfather's property. The village was a small hamlet; it had no school and young boys of the village had to walk for miles through the fields to attend school in a neighbouring village. It was when Harish Boodhoo announced that he would make a contribution for school books for the young students of the village that the attitude of the villagers changed. Boodhoo's relatives embraced him and other villagers came forward to welcome him. Harish Boodhoo visited his village a few years later, his journey was much more comfortable the second time for he travelled on *pucca* road which was named in his honour.

Gauitra Bahadur's cousins also asked inquisitive questions of her escort on whether she had any designs on the family land. Gauitra made two trips and one of the questions that dogged her, though never openly articulated to her personally, was one that several descendants of the early migrants have faced during their visits to the ancestral home. The unexpressed apprehension in the minds of the relatives about the visitor is 'what does she want – does she want a share in the land?' Gauitra wrote in an article in the Hindustan Times (March 1, 2009) that her *Bihari* fourth cousins thought that she may covet the land. Gauitra did covet something she said, but what she was looking for as a writer was a narrative. The narrative she sought was her great-grandmother's narrative, the cousins' narrative and her own narrative, she explained.

Another returning *pravasi* Indian found the happy reunion had cooled a little after the young second cousin had called his elder brother in Mumbai to tell him the news. The city-dwelling brother had warned them to be wary of this unannounced visitor and her motives.

In one of the moving passages in the book, '*The Swinging Bridge*', Ramabai Espinet[6] wrote about Uncle Peter's unnerving experience with the village folk in India. Uncle Peter found that he was welcomed, acknowledged and offered sweets but was not allowed into the inner sanctum of the family fold and affection. Ramabai Espinet drew an evocative picture of Uncle Peter reaching his ancestral village together with an interpreter, of the excitement as the villagers, young and old gathered around him and the curious ritual with the oldest man in the village.

Relating the story to his family back home in Trinidad over one of the family lunches, Uncle Peter explained that "everyone" in the vicinity rushed to gather around him. Then the oldest man motioned for silence and sat down under an old neem tree. Uncle Peter followed suit and sat down opposite the old man on the dirt floor.

The old man picked up a stick and drew a circle in the dust before him; he then drew a smaller circle within the first circle and added a question mark in the centre. He looked towards the interpreter and started asking questions; Peter answered the questions through the interpreter. After a little while the old man got up and turned towards Uncle Peter and formally embraced the visitor. "Now we can close the circle", the old man said and he rubbed out the drawings in the dirt with his foot.

Uncle Peter was beside himself with emotion, related Ramabai Espinet. The women of the house came out to offer Uncle Peter tea and chappatis, but Uncle Peter only wanted to cry and hold those people close. But none of the villagers made any move towards him or tried to touch him. They asked him no questions about himself, his home or his family. As Uncle Peter left the village, no one invited him to come again nor did they say anything about his children. They were satisfied, Espinet wrote, the circle had been closed. The family tree was complete, the missing members were accounted for and the circle was closed.

The reunion was emotionally wrenching for Uncle Peter, cataclysmic even. He was left hurt and perplexed by the response of the old man and the other relatives. The lack of engagement left him disconcerted and troubled. Those people had displayed anxious anticipation at first, but then they wanted their lives to go on as usual. Uncle Samuel consoled Uncle Peter saying they didn't mean to offer any offence; they were just simple people who did not think some one like Uncle Peter would want to see them again. "Ain't they close the circle. That was their way of accepting you," Uncle Samuel consoled.

Espinet has captured one of the myriad ways in which people in Indian villages respond to forgotten relatives and connections who come in from distant places. There is joy, out-pouring of affection, sometimes apprehension that the new-comer would want a share in the land, there are expectations from the foreign relative, at other times there is a disconnect with the stranger.

For others, the bare information of the existence of the relatives in a far-off place is enough; there is no desire to maintain the ties with the distant connections. Jagdeo's relatives flatly refused to believe that they had relatives across the globe; it was eventually the curiosity of the younger relatives which wrought some change in their attitude.

Former Prime Minister of Trinidad, Basdeo Panday spoke of his own experience in visiting his ancestral home and meeting relatives during a seminar in Delhi. "Finding one's roots is an experience which words cannot convey," said Basdeo Panday. "Seeking one's roots is a deeply psychological yearning. And one has to be prepared for it. It can be painful to find your relatives in poverty. And how one has to relate to the newly-found family is something one has to deal with, too," he added. Most of the relatives in the ancestral villages are village folk with a bit of land or a small business.

Minal Hajratwala wrote about Bharati, her first cousin, the only one of her 36 first cousins who remained in India and the family's expectations. Bharati lived in Kalyaan, north of Mumbai; her son, Jayant dreamt of migrating to America. Minal stayed in touch with Jayant through email. "At first his emails are affectionate, eventually, when I proved impotent as a gateway to America, his messages took an aggressive turn. 'You come and eat my food, I hope my interview helpful,' he wrote bitterly. Then they became abusive and I stopped writing back. .... I feel sympathy for his dilemma, for his clear sense of betrayal. The implicit promise of my American presence in his life, my friendliness and empathy, was that I could help him, too, to become an American. That I cannot is a matter for legitimate frustration, even rage," Minal wrote.

The majority of relatives welcome the stranger into their house and it is the beginning of a relationship. However, there is the possibility that the roots seeker locates the ancestral village but does not find any relatives. Indian villages are changing; there is a considerable amount of migration to urban areas, so it is not always possible to discover relatives. But, even for those who do not find relatives, a visit to the ancestral village is an emotional experience.

Praveen Chandra went to Bhatwari kalan village but found no relatives. He wrote about his visit: "As I got up to go, I touched the bright soil at my feet and wondered if there was an old tree or rock I could touch in the hope that my great-grandfather had done the same more than a century ago."

Notes

1. '*Bittersweet: Voices from the Past*' by Praveen Chandra and Saras Chandra, edited by Brij V Lal, Pandanus Books.
2. *Finding the West Indies in India*, a mongraph by Nalini Mohabir.
3. *The First Crossing*, edited by David Dabydeen, J Morely, B Samaroo, Amar Wahab & B Wells, The Derek Walcott Press, 2007.

4. http://www.kpspublications.com/Discoveringroots
5. *Lineages and Linkages, Solving Trinidad Roots in India* by Shamshu Deen, S Deen, 1998.
6. *The Swinging Bridge* by Ramabai Espinet, HarperCollins.

High Profile Searches: Basdeo Panday, Bharrat Jagdeo, Navin Ramgoolam

The search for roots is an intensely personal longing among the people of Indian origin living in the former British or French colonies. But the issues of loyalty to the country of birth and settlement dampened this yearning for many years. In multiracial societies like Fiji, Trinidad and Guyana, Indian minorities have often had to face charges of harbouring dual loyalties. Any sentimental yearning for the old homeland even three generations after the act of migration could be seen as slightly disloyal. The difficulties associated with trying to trace one's ancestor's passage to the new home also acted as a deterrent for many overseas Indians.

The situation changed after the discovery of the ancestral village homes of top leaders of these countries. It was no longer disloyal to display an affinity to the ancestral homeland and more and more overseas Indians expressed a desire to search for their own roots. Bharrat Jagdeo, President of Guyana referred to that view when he returned home to Georgetown after visiting his ancestral village in India. Jagdeo said: "I am very proud of my ancestry. I am a born Guyanese and as president of the nation I have utmost loyalty to Guyana. At the same time, I am extremely proud that I am an Indian-origin. I do not see any conflict."

Basdeo Panday was elected as Prime Minister of Trinidad and Tobago in 1995; he was the first person of Indian origin to hold the high post. Eminent genealogist, Shamshu Deen had a project to carry out a roots search in India for twenty Trinidad families, and among the twenty cases Deen took up was a search for Basdeo Panday's ancestral home. Shamshu Deen had gone through the records in the National Archives in Port of Spain and consulted other documents. The emigration pass stated that Basdeo Panday's ancestor had come to Trinidad from a village in Azamgarh district. In 1997 when the Indian government invited Basdeo Panday to be the chief guest at the Republic Day celebrations a visit to Lachmanpur village was included in the official programme.

Basdeo Panday's grandparents, Ajodhia and Subhanti left their home in Lachmanpur village in 1908 and went to Trinidad on the ship, Ganges. A year later, Subhanti's mother, Laganee reached Trinidad in search of her daughter. Subhanti was a woman of means and she came as a fare paying passenger on the ship, Indus and bought an estate in Trinidad.

Basdeo Panday's ancestor, Ajodhia belonged to Lachmanpur village of Kandhorapur *thana* in Azamgarh district. Ajodhia's father was Niharoo and his next of kin as listed in the emigration pass was his nephew, Ramkishun. *Thana* Kandhorapur did not have a village called Lachmanpur under its jurisdiction but there were a number of similar sounding village names in the region – Lakshmanpur and its variations is as common a name as Rampur in the northern states. But there was no trace of the family of an *ahir* caste man, who had gone abroad in these villages. The search went further afield to a tiny hamlet called Lachmanpur in the next *thana*. A visit to the Tabatpur *thana* revealed that it was a new *thana* that had been established in 1982. At Lachmanpur – Tabatpur, a 70-year old man, Baggal recalled that his grandmother had told him that his grandfather's uncle had gone away. His grandfather's name was Ramkishun and he had an ancestor whose name was Niharoo!

By the time Basdeo Panday came to visit his ancestral village, Lachmanpur had been spruced up fit to receive a Prime Minister. But it was a very emotional experience for Panday; he broke down and wept. It was a moving experience to come home and see the land from which the family had been displaced. Basdeo Panday is said to have looked at one of the ladies welcoming him to the village and exclaimed: "You resemble my mother!"

The Pandays visit to their home in Azamgarh led to several other people making efforts to seek their connections to India. The National Archives of Trinidad also took up a programme to place the emigration passes and the ship's registers on microfilm for easy access.

President of Guyana, Bharrat Jagdeo's experience was similar to Basdeo Panday's story. Jagdeo was to visit India in 2003 on a state visit. As the plans for the President's visit were being charted out, his office informed the Ministry of External Affairs in New Delhi that President Jagdeo would like to start his first visit to India from the village that his ancestors had left to come to Guyana. It was an emotional desire and when the President's wish was conveyed to the External Affairs Ministry in Delhi, it set in motion the process of locating the village – Thakurain ka purwa.

The Ministry of External Affairs got in touch with the Uttar Pradesh state government which directed the district administration to look through its records. There were about a dozen villages in Uttar Pradesh with 'thakura' as part of the name, either as a prefix or a suffix. Village names have undergone some changes and the information sent by the Guyana High Commission was not very clear on the name. The officials first reduced the list to three names after examining the other villages. In each of the three villages, the officials talked to the villagers, especially the elderly residents of the village.

According to the district magistrate, MP Agarwal, oral histories were collected in each of the villages, and while speaking to the older people in Thakurain ka purwa, the search team heard about a couple who had left to go abroad. A little later, one elderly villager recalled that the person who had gone away was named Ram Jiyawan. It was the name of Bharrat Jagdeo's grandfather! After some further questioning and meeting other villagers, the team concluded that they had identified President Jagdeo's ancestral village.

Thakurain ka purwa is located about 150 kms from the state capital, Lucknow; the district has been renamed and is now known as Chatrapati Sahuji Maharaj Nagar. The village was a small hamlet off the main road, with only a narrow dirt road connecting it. Thakurain ka purwa village was shaken out of its usual sleepy existence when a group of senior government officials descended on it to verify if it was the very same village. It was galvanised into action over the next couple of weeks as the district administration gave the village a face-lift and made preparations to receive a presidential visit. The dirt road was quickly widened and made into a tar-sealed road for the convoy of cars carrying state leaders and officials. A helipad was prepared in a vacant field for the Indian Air Force helicopter carrying the President of Guyana to land at a site close to the village.

Excitement reigned high in the entire region over the visit, particularly after word spread that the high dignitary had especially asked to begin his visit to India from the village of his ancestors. People were deeply moved by the sentiment. Men, women and youngsters from the neighbouring villages crowded into Thakurain ka purwa on a hot day in August, 2003 – they had come to catch a glimpse of the *rashtrapati* (president), who valued his ties to his ancestors and wanted to pay homage to his forefathers.

As he arrived at the village, Bharrat Jagdeo was welcomed by his relatives who offered garlands and sweets. Jagdeo responded by hugging them and patting the young children on the head. He was then taken to meet his oldest surviving relative, Ram Dulari. Ninety-year-old Ram Dulari was the sister of Ram Jiyawan, Jagdeo's grandfather who had gone to Guyana. Ram Dulari held onto her grandnephew's hands as he bowed down to greet her. "He looks and behaves just like us", was the reaction of the boys and girls who crowded around the guest.

Ram Dulari vividly recalled Ram Jiyawan, who had gone away with his wife. She said that Ram Jiyawan had done the right thing to leave Thakurain ka purwa and go away to find work, since there was so much poverty in the village. Now his grandson is rashtrapati of a country, she added. She handed over a slip of paper to the President , asking for a job for her grandson, repairs to the roof of the house and a factory to be set up near the village to provide employment for the youth. It was the kind of petition that villagers hand over to visiting politicians and senior officials. To Ram Dulari, Jagdeo was a president so he could do anything.

"I am emotional ... it is a humbling experience," Jagdeo told reporters as he reached his ancestral home. "Today, I think about my grandfather who had left the village – what was going in his mind at that time, I do not know. He was a brave man," Jagdeo added. He was taken to a spot in the village which he was told had been set aside for his grandfather, Ram Jiyawan. The land was built over, but Bharrat Jagdeo lit a lamp at that spot in memory of his grandparents. Jagdeo's relatives, mainly cousins and second cousins presented him with a shawl and copies of the Ramayana and Bhagwad Gita.

On a later occasion in Georgetown, Bharrat Jagdeo talked about his mother's family. "My mother is from Chennai but my father was from Uttar Pradesh. I went to my father's village and found details of ancestors, but could not do that with my mother's side. I still have to do much more research on my mother's side from Chennai. My mother used to mention about Tamil Nadu and its rich heritage as my grandmother died before I was born. We have lost all the connections and roots. The only contact is soul-like contact and though you do not understand Hindi, you like the movies that are from India. When I came back from India, hundreds of people called me and asked how they could find their roots and needed my help in that direction."

The Guyanese President had inaugurated a 'Discover Your Roots' programme of the Uttar Pradesh government during that visit. The programme has had some success in locating ancestral homes of people of Indian origin, but much depends on the kind of information that is made available.

When Prime Minister of Mauritius, Navinchandra Ramgoolam was to visit India on an official visit in 2008, a visit to the village of his ancestors in the state of Bihar was high on the Mauritius leader's itinerary. Bihar's Chief Minister, Nitesh Kumar had visited Mauritius the year before. During his visit, the Chief Minister had met many people who had spoken about their wish to search for their roots, especially those whose forefathers came from Bihar. Nitesh Kumar had said that his government would collaborate with the government of Mauritius to prepare a database of all persons who had migrated from Bihar to Mauritius in an effort to help them trace their roots. It was to be part of a programme to foster closer cultural and economic ties between Bihar and Mauritius.

The Bihar government initiated a 'search for roots' programme with a search for Navin Ramgoolam's village. There were just a few details available about his family; his ancestor had come from village called Harigaon in the Bhojpur district of Bihar in the year, 1871. The Bihar government's department of culture was assigned the task of locating Harigoan village. However, locating Navin Ramgoolam's ancestral village was not an easy task. There were few details available, and once it became public knowledge that the Bihar government was seeking to locate Harigoan, the ancestral village of the Prime Minister of Mauritius, there was a flurry of activity. About 20 claimants emerged, who asserted that the Mauritius leader's ancestor had belonged to their village according to the popular mythology in the region.

It was a painstaking task to shift through the records and the oral history of the area and check on the authenticity of each of the claims. A few of the claims could be dismissed since the migrant's departure date did not match. One of the claims was more credible for it had the same name. The villagers produced the *'vanchavali'* – the village inheritance record that forms part of the revenue record to show that one Ramgulam Ojha from that village had gone to Mauritius. Ramgulam Ojha was claimed to be the ancestor of Sir Seewoosagar Ramgoolam, the towering leader of Mauritius who led the country to independence and the father of Prime Minister Navin Ramgoolam. The village, which was also called Harigaon was in Arrah district, Bihiya pargana. But the name of Mr Ramgoolam's ancestor, who went to Mauritius, was Moheeth, so the claim was rejected. Fortunately there was only one village named Harigaon in Bhojpur district and the sub-division revenue records listed the name of Moheeth. This was clinching evidence as Moheeth or Mohit was the name of the Ramgoolam family ancestor who had gone to Mauritius.

A tour of Harigaon in Bihar became an important part of Prime Minister Navin Ramgoolam's programme. Bihar's Chief Minister, Nitesh Kumar took personal interest in the arrangements for the visit and even accompanied the high dignitary to his ancestral village. Harigaon was dressed up in a new coat of paint with colourful buntings and banners welcoming the visitor on the day Navin Ramgoolam came home to his ancestral village. The village had received a quick makeover in the past few weeks. Chief Minister Nitish Kumar had toured the village once it was confirmed that it was the Harigoan listed on Moheeth's emigration pass. A new road was built connecting the village to the main road, a brand new health centre had been constructed and a few solar powered street lights had been put up in the village.

It was a poignant moment for Navin Ramgoolam and his wife, Veena as they entered Harigaon village. Ramgoolam bent down, touched the ground and picked up the dust to place on his forehead. The jubilant villagers roared their approval and the village elders and *panchayat* officials rushed forward to garland a 'son of the soil'.

After a rousing reception by the villagers, Navin Ramgoolam laid the foundation stone for a new school in the village. A little later, Chief Minister Nitish Kumar who had accompanied the Mauritius Prime Minister to Harigaon laid the foundation stone for a hospital to be named after Navin Ramgoolam. The village pond which had been cleaned up with a new *ghat* was named after his ancestor, Mohit Ramgoolam.

"It is like a festival for the villagers. After all, a grandson of the village, who became Prime Minister in a foreign country, is visiting Harigoan to pay respects to his roots," exclaimed a villager. In an effort to assuage the feelings of the other villages which had put forward a claim to the Ramgoolam ancestry, the Chief Minister announced that similar development of new tarred roads, schools and health centres would be constructed at each of the villages.

It was a grand homecoming, and at a function in Patna, Navin Ramgoolam described Bihar as his "motherland". He announced a gift of US $250,000 for a hospital in his ancestral village and an annual scholarship for two students from the state. Navin Ramgoolam unveiled a bronze statue of his father, Sir Seewoosagur Ramgoolam, at Patna's Gandhi Maidan. The nine-foot high, 600-kg statue had been created by well known sculptor, Anil Kumar Suthar. The Bihar government acknowledged Sir Seewoosagar Ramgoolam (he was prime minister of Mauritius from 1962 to 1982) as an illustrious son of Bihar, and declared that his birthday would be marked by a state function every year.

The story of Navin Ramgoolam's visit to his ancestors' home village raised the hopes of many other people in Mauritius. The Bihar Roots Foundation was set up with the aim to help connect Mauritians of Bihari origin to the land of their ancestors and preserve their ancestral language, Bhojpuri. The Bihar Foundation aims to connect Bhojpuri speakers around the world and to preserve the Bhojpuri language which is beginning to lose ground to Hindi and Creole language. Though many people of Indian origin speak Bhojpuri in Mauritius, the younger generation is getting more fluent in Hindi because of the influence of the popular Hindi film industry. The Prime Minister's visit to Harigaon sparked off an interest and several people wrote to the Bihar government with details of their grandparents, seeking help in searching for their ancestral connections to Bihar.

A young film maker, Shundell Prasad made a documentary film titled *Once More Removed* about her own search for her roots in India. Her film spans three different geographical regions. It starts from the Indo-Caribbean neighbourhoods in Queens, the New York immigrant area and goes back to Guyana where Shundell was born and then to the towns and districts from where her ancestors began their journey of migration. Shundell's family left Guyana and moved to the United States in the 1980s when the stagnant economy in Guyana forced many Guyanese of African and Indian origin to begin migrating to the US for jobs and better economic prospects. In India, Shundell travelled to Kolkata, and Muzzafarpur district in Bihar and Azamgarh district in Uttar Pradesh to shoot film and talk to different people.

Shundell Prasad's film was shown at the Pravasi Bharatiya Divas held in Hyderabad, Andhra Pradesh. While making the film, she met and spoke to many people. In an interview to a newsmagazine, Shundell spoke of her meeting with Bharrat Jagdeo, President of Guyana who had himself visited his ancestral village in Uttar Pradesh, and told her about his experience. She said that he had advised her on the need for careful cross checking and referencing so that she did not follow wrong leads.

The film showed Shundell finding her way to the ancestral villages of her parents, where she meets some distant relatives. Talking about her first meeting with her distant relatives, Shundell said, "At first I was speechless, I felt silly, I had searched so much and finally I was there. And I had nothing to say." But the women of the village took her in as one of their own – some of them touched her feet, others smiled at her in welcome.

Shundell Prasad was shocked at the poverty she saw in the village. Basdeo Panday had also referred to the subject when he said that one needed to be prepared for meeting one's relatives. "It can be painful to find your relatives in poverty. And how one has to relate to the newly-found family is something one has to deal with, too," he said. While the migrants were forced to find ways to make a living in a foreign land, those left behind lived on in the same home and faced few changes in the pattern of their village lives.

Family history searchers have had the satisfaction of visiting the ancestral homeland and identifying some of the landmarks that their ancestors spoke about. Twenty-five year old, Kullan Venkata Chetty had travelled to Natal from Madras port in 1909. Chetty's family landholding was not productive enough to sustain the family and Chetty decided to go with a group of other men to seek better economic opportunities. In Natal, Chetty was assigned to a dairy farm where he worked for five years. On completion of his contract Chetty decided to stay on in Natal; he worked at different kinds of jobs and finally started his own small business venture.

Kullan Venkata Chetty often spoke to his four sons about the small village in Tamil Nadu that was their ancestral home and told them to return to the family home. The Chetty family prospered in Natal and it was Gopaul, the youngest of the seven siblings who decided to go to India and try to trace their village home. In 2009, Gopaul and his sister, Nagamah travelled to Tamil Nadu and tracked down his father's family in Tiruvannamalai district. Gopaul and Nagamah went around the family's fields and saw the well and the temple exactly as their father had so often described to them. After discovering the family home, Gopaul has now begun trying to trace his mother's family, who belong to North Arcot district. Tiruvannamalai district, known for its Arunachaleswara temple and ashrams was once part of North Arcot district, till it was separated in 1989.

It is not only the descendants of indentured workers who are interested in reviving the India connection. Indians migrated to Malaya, Burma, East Africa; many of them went in search of work, others went as traders and merchants. Their descendants flourished in the new countries, and the ties with home faded over time. But a vague connection lingered on till it suddenly flickered into a stronger emotion.

Neera Kapur Dromson,[1] an Oddisi dancer living in Paris, wrote about her own journey of discovery in her book, '*From Jhelum to Tana*'. Neera had met her French husband while she was teaching dance at the French cultural centre in Nairobi. She had a bad back and was laid up in bed with time on her hands when she started thinking about her family background. It was a question her husband had asked that set her thinking. Where is your family from? – he had asked. India was not home, Neera thought, she had been to India earlier and there was no sense of homecoming. So where was home, she wondered.

About a year later Neera went home to Nairobi and asked her mother about the family history. Her mother showed her a picture of her great grandfather – Lala Kriparam Lalchand. The portrait had been painted by an Italian prisoner-of-war who had been interred with him during World War II. Looking at the picture of her great grandfather sitting stiffly on a chair made Neera realise that she knew very little about this intrepid ancestor. Who was he and why did he leave his family home to journey out to Mombasa, Kenya and how did he make his life in that country, Neera asked herself.

When Neera began looking for books that would give the history of the Indian community in Kenya, she discovered that there was no written material available about the Indians presence in Kenya, on how the Indians arrived in Kenya and the experiences they went through to make a living in the new country. Neera began to try and learn about the family history but came up against the fact that Indians do not write diaries or preserve old documents. So she looked for elderly people to ask them their stories, the oral histories and anecdotes. But many of them were reluctant to talk about the old days – especially the difficult times they had faced. "People don't want to talk, they want to keep the old scandals buried, others don't want to be reminded of bad times," Neera said.

She began talking to older people in the family and letting them reminisce about old events; some were garrulous while others were reluctant to talk especially about the bad times. They did not want to open up old resentments or scandals that were safely buried. Finally, it was her mother and her grandaunt who understood her need to know and opened up to her questions.

Though it was not difficult to travel between India and Kenya, neither her parents nor her grandparents had any sense of connection to India nor did they keep in touch with relatives in the ancestral village. Neera's great grandfather's village had become part of Pakistan after Partition. Neera did not know what Partition meant so she learnt about the history of the Indian sub-continent and the partition of India into two countries, India and Pakistan at the time of independence. But it was important for Neera to make the reverse journey from Tana, the small town where her grandfather had set up shop to the little village of Maine near the Jhelum River. Her great grandparents came to Kenya, from Maini and Bhera, two villages not too distant from each other that lie in north-west Punjab in Pakistan. Finally there was a chance to go to Pakistan when Neera's husband was posted to Delhi. Neera grabbed the opportunity and reached Lahore.

A tortuous road journey brought her to Maine but there were no Hindus living in Maine. However, the old havelis were intact and their paintings well preserved. The havelis had names painted on them like Chadha Haveli or Krishna Nivas. "And the people were so receptive to me, as a lost sibling has come home. I had never felt it in India – the tears and the laughter. It was a feeling that I had touched my hand to the soil – I had come home."

Neera wrote of how important roots were, she could not feel herself as Indian, and in Kenya she was not seen as Kenyan. Going to Maine she came to understand that "identity is not fixed, it is an ongoing process. My identity will keep on growing. I feel a citizen of the world, and can feel comfortable anywhere. I am coming to terms with myself."

New York city resident, Mira Kamdar also made a voyage of discovery, tracing her family's multiple migrations. In her book, '*Motiba's Tattoos*'[2], Mira Kamdar wrote about her grandmother's (universally known as Motiba) journey – a journey that started from a small, dusty village in Gujarat's Rajkot district and went through Burma to Bombay and then to America.

Motiba, named Jayakunver Khara, was born in 1908 in Gokhlana, a small village in Kathiawar in the state of Gujarat. Mira's grandfather, Prabhudas had gone to Rangoon and became a highly successful businessman in Burma, but had to leave Burma during the war. The family returned after the war was over but Prabhudas was expelled by the Burmese government during the crackdown on Indians. The family settled in Bombay and Mira's father was sent to the United States to study in 1949. Mira Kamdar grew up in America.

A few years before her death, Motiba's thoughts began to run towards Gokhlana. She had left the village as a five-year old and had never returned, but she wanted to make one last visit. She could never make that trip, but after her death, Mira resolved to go to Gokhlana in her Motiba's memory. Mira, accompanied by her father and Motiba's brother's wife, Dhirajben drove in a hired car to Jasdan, the small town nearest to Gokhlana. The maps they carried did not show Gokhlana and they had to stop to ask for directions. But most of the people they asked in Jasdan had not heard of Gokhlana, finally they found one man who knew the road and pointed them to the right direction.

They reached the village and walked down the dirt road to the open space in front of the village temple. A group of middle aged villagers sitting under a tree in the village square watched the newcomers impassively till Mira's father said in the local Kathiawari dialect: "This is our village. Our family is Khara and we used to live here. Can you show us our old house?" It sent a frisson of excitement through the old men, who jumped up to welcome the Kharas. A small group formed up to show them around the village. They were welcomed into the old Khara house by the brahmin family who had been gifted the house by Mira's great grandfather. The oldest member of the family remembered Motiba and showed them the set of rooms where her parents had lived and Motiba was born. The trip was Motiba's way of connecting her beloved granddaughter to the family's past.

Canadian politician, Ujjal Dosanj left his village, Dosanj kalan in the Phagwara district of Punjab as a young lad. He travelled to Britain and then to Canada to settle down in Vancouver. He went on to become the Premier of the province of British Columbia and later a Member of Parliament. After a visit to his village in 2005, Ujjal Dosanj remarked, "One's connections to the land of one's ancestors, forefathers is eternal. It cannot be broken, it runs too deep."

Thelochan Balgobind, a South African entrepreneur was interested in his family's antecedents from a young age. As he was growing up in South Africa, the grandson of indentured workers was keen to know more and more about his family in South Africa and in India. This desire grew into an urge to learn about the family history and trace its roots back in India. It was not an easy task but slowly and surely Thelochan managed to trace his grandfather, Mahilall's native home and helped build bonds with the relatives in the old village.

In a series of interviews with his daughter, Shanta Balgobind Singh, a Professor of Criminology at the University of KwaZulu-

Natal, Thelochan Balgobind related his experiences while searching for the family's roots. He explained that his paternal grandfather, Mehi Sahu, later known Mahilall came to South Africa as an indentured labourer in 1883. Mahilall was indentured to the Waterloo Estate on the north coast of Natal for five years; he married Bechuni Kallichuran, whose parents had also come to South Africa from Bihar state. On completing his indenture term, Mahilall leased some dry, uncultivated land in the New Glasgow area and planted sugarcane on it. Mahilall and Bechuni stayed on in Natal and had 14 children of whom ten were sons and four daughters. One of their sons was Balgobind, who was Thelochan's father. As it became necessary in the colonial society to have a surname and a given (first) name instead of the single name that most of the indentured workers used, Thelochan came to be known as Thelochan Balgobind.

Thelochan began meticulous efforts to search his family history. He knew his family name and the year his grandparents had arrived in South Africa. He visited the Durban Archives Repository to obtain information on the Indian arrival in Natal. At the Archives he searched through documents and located the ship's list of immigrants for the ship, Sophia Jaohim on which his grandfather had travelled to Natal. The ship's passenger list gave some crucial information – Mahilall was 25 years of age when he arrived in Natal on 14 August 1883, and his colonial number as listed in the ship's record was 29953. His caste was *sonar* (goldsmith) and his village was given as Hurpurwa in Sarlahi district of Bihar.

In 1971, Thelochan Balgobind began his journey to his roots – a journey that has been termed a "pilgrimage" by many other roots seekers. Reaching the actual village in India was an arduous task. As Thelochan tellingly described it: "First you have to get to India, with the passenger list – it has the village, state, full address. You have to go to the biggest place first, the nearest city, and there you go to the government office, they know everything. You keep repeating the same thing in every city, until you get nearer and nearer, closer and closer."

His journey took him to many small villages on the India-Nepal border before he finally reached Hurpurwa. Thelochan described how he reached Hurpurwa together with his wife, Sonmathie, sister Domathie and brother-in-law, Kasipersad in the early evening and asked for the village *sarpanch* (the headman). The villagers brought out a clean sheet and spread it out on the floor for the visitors to sit. The *sarpanch* sent for a family from the *sonar* caste. Thelochan mentioned his grandfather's name and the villagers had an inkling about it. The *sonar* family said that they knew of an uncle who had disappeared without a trace from the village; their father had told them about the missing uncle – but that was all that they knew.

As it was getting late, Thelochan and his family stayed overnight at the village talking to the villagers till late hours. After much discussion and investigation, Thelochan and the *sarpanch* established that the *sonar* family were Thelochan's relatives. Thelochan stayed on for a couple of days to confirm that he was at the right location. "I was satisfied that I was in the right place," Thelochan Balgobind told Shanta.

"I was always cautious of people but after talking to the elderly people of the village I realized that the disappearance of my grandfather was a much talked about incident in the area." The village people were harmless, he said, timid and very calm and down to earth, he added. They were very inquisitive about the visitors; they wanted to know more and more. They don't even know where South Africa was. Thelochan said that on his second trip to the village he "took an atlas and maps and one of those inflatable globes which I subsequently left at the school."

After the first trip in 1971, Thelochan made ten more trips to Hurpurwa village and remained in regular touch with his Indian family. Thelochan Balgobind gave some money to his cousins for the school funds and temple funds on his first visit; on later trips he gave money for digging a borewell to supply water for the family.

Thelochan described the conditions in Hurpur village at the time of his first visit. Living conditions in the village were very poor, he said, the villagers lived in mud huts with thatched roofs, there was neither running water nor electricity in the village. His last trip to the village was in 2008, and by that time many changes had taken place and Thelochan found his relatives doing much better than before. The village had electricity and cell phones and the children were growing up and getting educated.

Over the years, Thelochan took his mother, brothers, sisters and other family members to the village. The families in two different parts of the world remain in regular touch with each other; the bonds of kinship have grown over the years. Thelochan Balgobind and his brothers helped one of their nephews with funds to go to America, where he obtained a green card. The nephew, Santosh Kumar now lives in America and sends money to his family in the village. Earlier Thelochan had sponsored another nephew to come to South Africa.

As Thelochan explained to Shanta Balgobind Singh, "the main thing is that you must have the desire to know who you are, where you come from, your true identity and origins. One must have the desire to do something and take the first step. Having traced my family in India I feel a sense of fulfilment. My cousins and uncles both in South Africa and the village are very proud of what I've done and achieved."

Notes

1. *From Jhelum to Tana by* Neera Kapur-Dromson, Penguin Books.
2. *Motiba's Tattoos: A granddaughter's journey into her Indian family's past* by Mira Kamdar, Public Affairs.

Girmitiya Stories from the Pacific: Rajendra Prasad, Satish Rai

The *girmit* (indenture) story has been largely forgotten in the countries where Indian workers lived. It is no longer a part of the Indian community's present day narrative. That strand of oral history is forgotten for the later generations tried to put behind them the painful era which the *girmitiyas* had described as *narak* (hell). But the story still has the power to stir up emotions among the descendants of the *girmitiyas* when they learn of the terrible days of servitude.

Rajendra Prasad, a descendant of Fiji *girmitiyas*, worked with the Fiji government and later migrated to New Zealand. Rajendra Prasad researched the history of Indians in Fiji and wrote a passionate account of the Indian experience in his book titled '*Tears in Paradise*'.[1]

Rajendra Prasad's grandparents, Bhudai and Dulara reached Fiji on the ship Sangola ll in 1908. They had travelled with Bhudai's cousin, Dhelai and his wife Changura. After completing their indenture contract, the two families leased a patch of land in Ba district in the heart of Fiji's cane growing area. The two families lived on the farm and together raised their children. Rajendra Prasad grew up on the farm; he was close to his grandfather, Bhudai who often spoke to him about the old days and told him stories of the lost home in a village in Basti district in India.

Rajendra Prasad's grandparents were unusual for their time, for unlike other *girmitiyas* who never spoke of their indentured period, Bhudai and Dulara spoke freely of their *girmit* experience. *Girmit* had become a social taboo among the Indian society, according to

Rajendra Prasad. "This part of the Indians' history was buried by the passage of time and the community made a conscious effort to obliterate it from its memory because of a stigma attached to it," he wrote. His grandfather's stories made a deep impression on Rajendra Prasad's mind.

In 1974 Rajendra Prasad was working as Town Clerk in Ba, when he was awarded an Indian government scholarship to attend a course on municipal management at the Indian Institute of Public Administration in Delhi. Before he left for India, Rajendra Prasad's father, Ram Lal asked him to try and locate their family in India. Ram Lal rummaged through a pile of old papers kept in a battered biscuit tin in the hope of locating a more specific address for the village but could not find anything. Travelling to India was a rare event in those days and a stream of relatives, friends and visitors came by to wish Prasad a safe journey. Many of them speculated about his chances of locating relatives in India. His father's last words while seeing him off at Nadi airport were "*Beta, dekhna agar ho saki to pariwaar walan ke pata lagana.*" (Son, if possible, try to locate our relatives)

Rajendra Prasad related his story of searching for his roots with great poignancy and emotion. He was initially anxious about setting out on his journey to India. He said that his anxiety was largely due to the political and civil unrest that prevailed in India at that time. He had a mental picture of India as unsafe for travellers. While attending his course in Delhi, Prasad met other participants who belonged to Kanpur and Lucknow in Uttar Pradesh, two cities close to his grandfather's village. But no one had heard of Belha Ragho village near Basti. As his course neared its end Prasad grew even more anxious at the thought of failing in his mission to locate the village.

It was at that time that a new participant arrived at the Institute. Shambhunath Tandon was the Public Relations Officer of Kanpur City Council; he was intrigued by the story of indentured Indians.

Tandan recalled that he had a classmate, who lived near Basti. Tandon wrote to Advocate Ram Kumar Khare asking him to locate Belha Ragho village and any members of Prasad's family still living in the village. He also asked Khare to find out the names of any of their relatives who had gone abroad. Prasad was keen to get the names since he had heard stories of other Fiji Indians who tried to locate their relatives in India and had been deceived by some crooked people.

Some days later, Tandan received a reply to his letter; it mentioned the names of Budhai and his wife Dulara and their only son, Ram Lal, and identified Dhelai and his wife Changura as people who had left the village to go abroad. The packet included letters written by Ram Lal in 1928, 1945 and 1948 together with family photographs. The letter also stated that if the person visiting India was the youngest son of Ram Lal, his name was Rajendra Prasad.

The letter written in 1928 was faded and tearing at the folds, but the letters written in 1945 and 1948 and the photographs, although browned with age, were better preserved. "I was astounded to see those letters. They carried a heart-wrenching message. To the family, they were a source of comfort and consolation. I realised that these letters must have meant more to them than our minds could comprehend. They were treasured like family jewels, evidence of torn links that symbolised the family's hope of restoring that connection somehow, sometime." Rajendra Prasad wrote.

Prasad's wife, Aruna joined him in India in the last few weeks of his tour. Prasad, Aruna and Tandon took an overnight train to Lucknow and then a *tonga* to the bus station. They caught a decrepit bus for a bumpy two-hour ride to Birpur Khairaniya. They got off the bus and walked to the residence of Advocate Ram Kumar Khare. At Khare's house they were offered cold drinks and sweets. Then, a tractor was brought to the front of the house, Prasad and

Aruna climbed on to a wooden platform fixed to the drawbars of the tractor. Khare got in the driver's seat while Tandon perched on the mudguard of the tractor. The tractor cut across lush green fields as they drove to Belha Ragho village.

A large expectant crowd awaited them at the village. It was a colourful scene with women in saris and men wearing dhotis, a few of them had shaven heads and a *churki* (top-knot). "There was a touch of eeriness as I came near my ancestral home. I felt a warm spiritual embrace which was guiding me to the source of my roots. My beloved Dadaji was no longer physically in this world but I felt he was leading me in spirit into the waiting arms of his anxious family.

"Aruna and I walked towards them with the solemnity that the occasion demanded. My mind was tuned to the sensitivity of the moment. Emotion welled in us as it did in the people around us. The atmosphere was electric. Khare introduced us to Sant Ram, son of Munmun, Dadaji's youngest brother. He was clean-shaven with a moustache, bearing some resemblance to my father, including the look that depicted him as a person of authority and intellect. He led us to the elders. We stood as the elders greeted me with hugs or shook hands. The matriarch identified herself as the sister-in-law of Dadaji. Aruna reverentially touched her feet. It was a tender moment. There was a lone wail from an elderly woman, which broke into uncontrolled crying amongst the large group of women. We could not hold back our own emotions. We sat outside the mud huts on the charpoy, sobbing. I lost my voice and tried to compose myself. All around me there was unrestrained crying and wailing, even the young children, unaware why they were crying. We met Munmun, who was blind and frail," Prasad said.

Two women came with basins of warm water to wash Prasad and Aruna's feet and dry them. After this ritual they were given a welcoming drink of fresh cow's milk to drink. There was no one in the *Ahir* (caste) family who would read and write, nor did the village have a school. When they received any letters, they took them to the local advocate's house several miles away and had the advocate or his son read out the contents to them.

The Prasads' heard the story of their ancestors' departure. "The family, like many others, was struggling to make ends meet. Many chose to leave their homes for employment or better opportunities in other parts of the country. Mostly individuals hatched these plans themselves. Families rarely consented to separation. Separation broke their hearts. Some families are still looking for those who disappeared without trace. Budhai and Dhelai made their plans without the knowledge of our parents. They were married at the age of 11 or 12 yrs."

"One night Buddhai and Dhelai told us that they were going to a religious function in the neighbourhood with their wives. They did not want us to go with them, nor did they want us to tell other family members of their plans. They assured us that they would return with their share of *prasad* (religious offerings). We accepted what they told us", one of the villagers said.

In the morning there was a frantic search for them. The village was agog with their disappearance and a variety of rumours spread regarding their whereabouts. Twenty years later, a letter arrived from Budhai, it said that they were in Fiji *tapu* and were working in the sugarcane fields. They remembered every family member and enclosed ten pounds with the letter, requesting that it be used for digging a common well for the family.

After the story was told, a huge elephant was brought around. Aruna and Rajendra Prasad climbed on to the back of the elephant and were taken for a ride around the village. "I asked to be taken to the *peepal* trees that my grandfather talked about. The *peepal* trees were a towering presence in the family enclave. They towered over every other tree and their size spoke of their age. In the powerful roots of the trees lay the roots of my family.

"We were taken away by the women of the family. The matriarch sent for coconut oil and massaged it onto our dry skins and dishevelled hair. The older women took turns as if it were a religious ritual that could not be neglected. They laughed and joked. They made us feel we were part of that great inheritance – an integral part of the family. Age, time, distance or country could not separate us," Prasad wrote.

Rajendra Prasad was shown the communal well, which had been dug with the money sent by Dadaji in 1928. The well not only quenched the villagers thirst but was also a shrine in the memory of Dadaji and his cousin, Dhelai.

Another group of people was waiting outside the house – they were not family but their family members had also left them in circumstances reminiscent of Prasad's grandparents. One of them said his relative had gone to Cheenidad. Several decades had passed but the hopes of finding the whereabouts of their kin still remained alive. They had come to meet the visitors in the hope that they could tell them about their relatives.

As Rajendra Prasad and Aruna left, the crowd of villagers followed their tractor for a considerable distance. Describing his journey to Belha Ragho village as a pilgrimage, Rajendra Prasad said: "I found a new joy and a new identity in my roots. It changed my life completely and I was clear in my mind that I was able to restore the broken family link. I came to accept that, although I was an individual, I was also part of a larger web that I could not ignore as it gave me an identity. From time to time I returned to these memories to relish them and to experience again the power and magnetism of my roots."

Documentary film maker Satish Rai is also a descendant of *girmitiyas* of Fiji Islands, who travelled to his grandparents village. Rai grew up in Fiji and later moved to London and then to Sydney, Australia. Unlike Rajendra Prasad who was able to meet up with people who could help him locate a small village in Uttar Pradesh, Satish Rai made a couple of unsuccessful attempts to locate his grandparents village before he could get accurate information about the location of the village in Balrampur district.

Satish Rai had a lingering desire to know more about his family and ancestors. Over the years his interest in the girmit system increased and he began trying to learn more about the *girmitiyas* and their descendants and their role in Fiji's history. He began by talking to his relatives, and seeking information about the family. Rai had collected some information about his grandparents, Sukhdeo and Gokuldei from his father's elder brother.

Satish Rai travelled to India and then went to Lucknow and to Basti district but was not able to make any headway in his search. On his first trip to India, Rai was not sure of how to go about his search, nor did he have the right kind of assistance of people familiar with the locale. A second trip to India and Uttar Pradesh in 1995 also did not yield any results.

In 2001 Satish Rai went to India, he was to make his first documentary film on former Fiji Senator Asha Singh's visit to her maternal and paternal grandparents homes in Uttar Pradesh. Rai went to Balrampur and other districts like Basti and Rae Bareilly from where men and women had gone to Fiji and the Caribbean. He had interviewed people who recalled the men who had left for foreign countries. He had even managed to speak to some journalists in Balrampur about his own quest. Sometime later he got information from them that his grandmother's village was near Utraula. He finally managed to visit his grandmother's village in Utraula, Balrampur, during another trip to India in 2004.

The film that Satish Rai shot during his visit to Utraula was featured in Rai's second documentary film: *Milaap: A Royal Discovery*. As a writer and a film maker, Satish Rai has the facility to make his search come alive, both in words and on camera. It is a story of painstaking research and effort which culminated in his meeting his uncle and other relatives from his grandmother's side of the family.

Satish Rai related his search odyssey in his own words. He said: "Talking to my uncle Dhanus I learnt that my *aja* (maternal grandfather) and *aji* (maternal grandmother) came to Fiji with their two children, Girdhari and Banwari. Banwari died soon after their arrival in Fiji, but Sukhdev and Gokuldei had six more children in Fiji. Bans Bahadur was the first-born in Fiji, followed by Dhanus Dhari, Chattar Dhari and Raj Dhari, the youngest of the sons. They also had two daughters who I just know as *badki* (elder) and *chotki* (younger) *fua (*father's sisters). Each of my uncles and aunts had an average of eight children each, except Chattar *kaka* (uncle), who never married and lived with Dhanus uncle all his life.

"I had thought about how I could trace my ancestral villages in India. I personally had no clue about which part of India they had come from. The books I read during my research for my novel provided important information about *girmityas* generally and in particular about those who had gone to Fiji. But it is one thing to know facts and figures, and it is a different ball game to try and trace one's own ancestors. In their wisdom the generations before me did not see it fit to document important information about our ancestors, especially about their homes and relatives back in India. At that time I did not have any clue about the *girmitya* emigration passes that were kept in the National Archives in Suva, Fiji," said Rai.

"The only person who recalled some information about *aja* and *aji* was Uncle Dhanus. I spoke to him over the phone from London where I was staying. At first Uncle Danush was not forthcoming with much information and he tried to dissuade me from 'digging up the past'. For some reason he was still very angry at his Uma *nana* (maternal grandfather). But he eventually did tell me a bit about his mother's history. He stated that his mother (my *aji*) came from district Gonda and thana, Utraula. He also mentioned Balrampur and that *aja* was from somewhere in Faizabad. He also said that my *aji's* father's name (his *nana*) was Uma Rai and that during the time of *girmit* they owned much land in India. He mentioned that I would not be able to trace my *aja's* place or relatives in India as the only relative they were in touch with (*aja's* brother) had died soon after *aja* and *aji's girmit* had been completed. That was all my uncle was prepared to tell me.

"Armed with this bit of information I made plans for my dream trip to India. A day before I caught my flight to India I called my brother, Pramod in Fiji to let him know about my trip. He then told me that our cousin, Jayant was in Delhi on a study trip with his family. I immediately called Jayant and arranged to stay with him at his rented flat in Hauz Khas in Delhi. From there I ventured out to Jalandar, some places in Uttar Pradesh and as far as Mumbai, in search of our favourite Bollywood stars.

"My quest also began to take shape from there. Fortunately Jayant had already been in touch with his paternal and maternal ancestral homes in Ghaziabad and Diwakarpur in Basti. Both his *girmitya* ancestors had kept in touch with their homes in Uttar Pradesh and the link had never got broken. I accompanied Jayant to his paternal ancestral home in Ghaziabad and spent two nights in the village. The visit was an exceptional one, and I captured some memorable moments with the boys in the village. This was my first interaction with descendants of the *girmityas'* family in India.

"Jayant could not accompany me on the visit to his maternal village in Diwakarpur in Basti. On this visit I also hoped to look for my *aji's* village in Gonda. But this trip was much longer and tougher. The train journey to Ayodhya was more than twelve hours. From there I was to find my way to Diwakarpur on my own, although Jayant gave me directions. I managed to find Diwakarpur but by the time I arrived at Jayant's relatives' house I was exhausted. After a short visit I returned to Ayodhya. After touring temples of Ayodhya, I went to Faizabad, it was one of the names Uncle Dhanus had mentioned. The next day I began enquiring about my *aji's* village in Gonda.

"Rickshaw drivers in India are generally a great source of information. I told one of them about my quest and he appeared very interested. His attitude towards me changed dramatically when I told him my great grandfather's name (*aja's* father) to him. Upon hearing the name, Uma Rai he promptly informed me that I was searching for a *bhumihar brahmin* family. That came as a shock to me because no one had ever talked about our family being *brahmin*. He told me that *bhumihar brahmins* were landowning *brahmins* as opposed to priestly *brahmins*. This information tied up with some other bits of information provided to me by my Uncle Dhanus.

"I was on the right track, I thought to myself. But the next information from the rickshaw driver stumped me. He told me that Utraula was about one hundred kilometres away and I would have a difficult time getting there. I had already experienced many difficulties in finding Jayant's relatives in Diwakarpur, even with reliable information in hand. I had to make a decision, whether to make the hazardous journey to Utraula with an off chance of finding my *aji's* village or head back to the safety of Jayant's home in Delhi.

"All alone in the vast expanse of the Uttar Pradesh plains I felt lost and extremely tired. I headed back to Delhi, leaving the quest for my *aji's* village to another time. I promised to be better prepared the next time. I said goodbye to Jayant and his family in Delhi and headed back to London. In London I worked to complete the final draft of the novel I was writing. I decided to go for novelty printing in India. The cost for printing in India was right and I would get another chance to trace my *aji's* village in UP.

"I made a trip to India in January of 1995; this time my brother, Prakash and his wife joined me from Fiji. He told me an Indian *pundit*, who was working in Fiji would accompany them to India and would assist us to trace our *aji's* village in UP. Since the pundit belonged to Uttar Pradesh I made no further attempts to get any further information about *aji's* village, relying upon the *pundit* to help us out. By the time I met up with Prakash and Bhabhi in Delhi, they had already been to the pundit's house in UP. But the *pundit* made no attempt to take them to *aji's* village.

"In fact throughout our stay in India he made no effort to take us to UP; he was quite content for us to pay for his accommodation and food. Completely disillusioned by his deceit I concentrated on publication of my novel. Once the novel was printed I returned to London. I was no nearer to finding my *aji's* village by the time I said goodbye to Prakash and Bhabhi, who returned to Fiji via Sydney.

"In the next few years, I wrote extensively on *girmit* for the Indo-Fijian papers in Sydney and made a feature film. I again decided to go to India and capture my next journey to Uttar Pradesh on camera. I knew I could reach Utraula this time. I was lucky that the Internet was around this time and I searched the net for information on Uttar Pradesh, Gonda and Utraula. Amazingly I found a page that read Discover Your Roots Project on UP Tourism Department's web page.

"I contacted the project in UP and I was promised some help in my quest to find my ancestral village and the proposed documentary film. As I was finalizing my trip to India my cousin, Asha emailed me from Fiji and stated that she wished to visit her relatives in UP. Asha, a senator in Mahendra Chaudhry's government at that time, is the sister of Jayant, who had returned to Fiji after completing his study in Delhi. I welcomed Asha's decision as her visit to her ancestral homes in UP would provide me excellent footage for my documentary. I was ready to shoot my first documentary.

"Asha, my producer Anju and I arrived in UP in January 2001. For seven days we travelled many miles in Uttar Pradesh shooting footage for the documentary. Asha's emotional pilgrimages to her ancestral villages in Ghaziabad and Basti were captured on my camera. We were fortunate to film visits to three other villages from where *girmityas* had gone to Fiji, Guyana and Mauritius.

"We were lucky to get acquainted with Dilip Singh, a neighbour of Asha's relatives in Basti. He became our guide in Basti and after the shoot there, took us to Utraula. Upon learning that I did not have any definite information, Dilip suggested that we should get assistance from the local press to trace my *aji's* village. When we reached Balrampur, which had now become a separate district from Gonda, he quickly organised a press conference for me. I gave the interview and departed for Delhi, knowing that it will take some time for the information to filter down to the local people. My third trip to India had come to an end and I was still short of finding my *aji's* village, let alone start searching for my *aja's* village.

"However, I was not disappointed with my third visit. I had a lot of footage for my first documentary film, had made some good contacts in UP as well as Bollywood. My knowledge of India and how to find my way around had increased a lot and I was convinced sooner or later I would seek out my *aji's* village.

"Back in my studio in the western suburb of Sydney, I completed production of my first documentary film '*Milaap-Discover Your Indian Roots*'. My documentary film Milaap had made an impression on Anil Oraw, the assistant director of Tourism India,Sydney. Anil had also come to know about my work in promoting Discover your Indian Roots project and invited me to join them for the inaugural India Week function being held in Fiji. The most revealing aspect of this week was the daily information sessions I held with India Tourism at the Civic Centre auditorium in Suva, the capital city of Fiji. Despite little publicity about the seminars, hundreds of Indo-Fijians came to the Civic Centre to get information on how to trace their ancestors in India.

"This much of interest in tracing their roots in India from the Indo-Fijians came as shock to us all. Anil and Raj, his colleague from India-Tourism, Sydney, were amazed to see so much interest among Indo-Fijians for their ancestral roots in India. People came from far; clutching whatever documentary information they had about their *girmitiya* ancestors. They were searching for their roots in Uttar Pradesh, Bihar, Rajasthan, Haryana, Punjab, Andhra Pradesh, Tamil Nadu and Kerala. Men, women, young, old, house wives, students, cane cutters and office workers all came to enquire about their ancestors. The response from the ordinary Indo-Fijians completely overwhelmed all of us. Towards the end of the week I spent a lot of time in the National Archives of Fiji, assisting people to look for their ancestors' *girmit* (emigration) passes, which contained the only definite information about their village, district, estate and next of kin in India. In all we saw some nine hundred people and assisted some one hundred of them to obtain copies of the *girmit* passes.

"Impressed with the success of the Milaap Project in Fiji, Anil and Raj recommended to the Government of India Tourist Office in Delhi to sponsor the shoot of my second documentary film on Milaap Project for January 2004. I started my shoot from Karauli, a town approximately half way between Jaipur and Agra. I regarded the Karauli shoot as a success for having traced a *girmitiya's* ancestral village within a day. This was a great shot in the arm for the project that lay ahead for me. I then reached Lucknow on a cold winter morning. For this part of my shoot, I was joined by Jainan Rai, a government approved tourist guide from Varanasi and a driver from UP Tourism. The four day shoot in UP was fast and full of excitement as well as disappointments. After handing over 60 immigration passes of Fiji *girmityas* to the Discover Your Roots Project now located in the new offices of Uttar Pradesh Tourist Department, we began our shoot, which covered Gonda, Balrampur, Utraula, Basti and Lucknow.

"The Utraula shoot was most important for me as finally I was going to the village where my *aji* was born. After some dramas on the way to Utraula I arrived in Shreedutganj, the town where we met up with my uncle and cousins. The meeting with my 94-year-old uncle, Dhoke Rai was a very emotional moment. And I fought hard to avoid embarrassing myself by crying in front of scores of people who had gathered around to witness this memorable reunion of blood relatives parted by fate some 96 years ago. The cousins then took us to Galibpur, and to the home where my *aji* was born and bred before she was married off in her teens to a Rai Bahadur of Faizabad.

"I had seen a picture of my *aji* and I felt at home as soon as I saw uncle Dhoke and my cousins. The family resemblance was striking and the tales they told me in the courtyard of my *aji's* childhood home were compelling. My *aji's* ancestors were the royal poets in the court of the Maharaja of Balrampur for which they were bestowed the title of Rai. They were also given several villages by the maharaja and hence the title *bhumihar brahmin*. The present prince of Balrampur confirmed this in an interview with me at the palace. My uncle Dhoke still gets a small pension from the royal palace, even after royalty was abolished many decades ago. The abolition of the royalty also meant that our family lost most of its land and they now survive mostly through business in Shreedutganj.

"Back in my *aji's* childhood home in Galibpur my own childhood puzzlement about the Rai family of Natabua (in Fiji) began to make sense. I realised that it must have been difficult for my *aji* to shake off her upbringing in Galibpur. Being part of the royal poet family, education must have been a priority for her children. Uncle Dhanus had told me that my *aja* had bought back her indenture from the Colonial Sugar Refining Company (CSR) after she fell pregnant one and a half years into her *girmit*.

"Sukhdev and Gokuldei's indenture period ended in 1921, which indicated that they were among the last batches of indentured workers to arrive in Fiji. Conditions on the plantations in Fiji were quite different by that time as the indenture system was on its last legs. Sukhdev was able to buy back his wife's indenture contract. That to me indicated the great love and respect my *aja* must have had for my *aji*; and the sacrifices he must have made to see *aji* retain semblance of a familiar way of life, despite the ravages of *girmit*," Satish Rai explained.

"Although I had obtained my *aja's* girmit pass from the National Archives in Fiji, I could not find his stated village or home in Basti. This reminded me what Uncle Dhanus told me about ten years ago. He was right about my *aja* not having any known relatives in India. I was very sad about that; I really wanted to know more about my *aja*, who made so many sacrifices to keep my *aji* happy. When I heard more about my *aji's* life from my newly found relatives in India, my respect for my *aja* grew further. At the end of my search I reconciled with the fact that I may never find his origins in India. But I haven't given up all my hopes yet," Satish Rai said.

Sometimes the village cannot be identified because the police station and the tehsil were written incorrectly or the ancestor had intentionally given wrong information at the time of signing the indenture contract. This was a not infrequent happening in the decades after the 1857 War of Independence, when the migrants were trying to evade the British authorities or were displaced from their homes due to punitive penalties imposed on their villages.

In Satish Rai's grandfather's case, the family in Fiji had lost contact after the one relative they were in touch with passed away. He could not discover why his grandparents migrated to Fiji when they belonged to prosperous families in India. But Dr Kamlesh Sharma came up against another kind of difficulty. Sharma was helping a friend locate his ancestor's emigration pass in the archives, but it was a futile search. Dr Sharma explained, "My friend's grandfather had changed his name to Din Mohammad from Din Dayal Sharma (to escape conviction for murder in India) prior to his migration to Fiji. My friend had no other details and there were about thirty other individual entries for Din Mohammed and Dean Mohammad in the register. As we had no idea what he would have recorded as his father's name that was the end of the search. The probability was that he would have faked all the other details on the immigration pass as well. This was a tragic end to the search. We would have been more successful if more vital data could be obtained from my friend's family but no one was prepared to share any information (for unknown reasons)."

Unlike Satish Rai, Shobha Rae was not much interested in family connections, she already had a host of cousins, uncles and aunts spread across several countries. Satish Rai and Shobha Rae are not related though Shobha was also born in Fiji. She had migrated to Canada and settled in Vancouver while her brother continued to live in Fiji, and she had cousins living in New Zealand and Australia. With having to keep in touch with family in four different countries, Shobha had little time to think of any connections with India.

Shobha's notions about family history underwent a great change in 2004 when she attended a book launch function. The book was *'Tears in Paradise'* by Rajendra Prasad; and Prasad's impassioned speech about indenture and tracing his ancestral village touched a chord. Shobha recalled, "The speech really moved me. All those years ago, I was not interested in the family, but now I wanted to know about my own ancestors and their lives. It really made me want to find my own roots and learn more about my family."

Shobha Rae explained that she had not known much about indenture before she read Rajendra Prasad's book. "We did not learn anything about indenture in school in Fiji. We were taught British history, European history but we did not hear anything about our own history. About how our forefathers were brought to Fiji and how they lived. Now I wanted to know more about the subject," Shobha exclaimed.

Shobha Rae began a quest for her family roots that year. Some years back, she had shown no interest in her father's story of his visit to the ancestral village in India, but Shobha recalled, "Things happen when they are meant to." Her father, Rajendra Rae had visited the ancestral village in 1987 and had returned to Fiji and told his children and other relatives about his trip. Shobha and her cousins did not find the story overly exciting, though she had written down the family tree, addresses and other details as her father related them. "At that time I was not much interested in all this. My father told me to write it down, so I wrote it and then forgot all about it."

Later that year Shobha went to Fiji to attend the centenary celebrations of the founding of the Arya Pratinidhi Sabha; her grandfather had been one of the founders of the Arya Samaj in Fiji in 1904. It was Bhairon Rae, Shobha's grandfather, who had left the village in Uttar Pradesh and gone to Fiji Islands across the seven seas.

Shobha and her brother, Promod Rae, who is a politician in Fiji, paid a visit to the National Archives to learn about their grandfather. They scrolled through the Archives database to locate their grandfather's emigration pass. By 2004, the search for the emigration pass was made much easier at the National Archives. The Indian indenture immigration list had been digitised and was now available on the computer. Earlier searchers had been severely constrained in making searches because the lists were bound in folios based on the year and ship of arrival.

It was about that time when other members of the family were also getting interested in the family history. Shobha could not find the piece of paper where she had jotted down the information her father had given her after his return from India. But when she wrote to her cousin, Nirmala in New Zealand about how she had obtained a copy of her grandfather's emigration pass, Nirmala had a pleasant surprise for her. Nirmala had also heard Rajendra Rae's story of his trip to India and put it down in a computer file; she could easily email it to her cousin. Nirmala's mail had an address for Ram Naresh Rai, a cousin of Rajendra Rae, whom he had met in Gorakhpur. (The Rae family in India spelt their surname as Rai)

Shobha wrote to the address but got no response. There was also a neighbour's phone number, but after getting through with some difficulty to that number Shobha learnt that the Rais no longer lived at that address. Also, there was no forwarding address.

Shobha eventually hired a researcher in India who travelled to Baijudhia village and talked to some people. He sent Shobha the address of Banwari Rai who had moved to Gorakhpur. Shobha wrote a letter to Banwari Rai in Hindi. By that time, Shobha was quite emotionally involved in her search and she waited anxiously for a response to her letter. One day when Shobha returned home for lunch from her office, the first thing she looked at was the pile of mail pushed in through the letter flap. Sorting through the junk mail, she saw the envelope with the Indian stamps. It contained a letter from Banwari Rai in Hindi and a short note in English from his grandson, Ranjit.

Tears started streaming from her eyes as she read the letters, recalled Shobha. "I was overtaken by my emotions, I cried and cried as I read and re-read the letters. I am getting goose bumps even now while thinking of that moment." She rang up the phone number her relatives had sent and talked to them.

It was from Banwari Rai that Shobha learnt that her grandfather had already been married when he went to Fiji; he left behind a wife and a baby boy. Bhairon Rai had married again and his second family in Fiji had no knowledge of his first marriage. Her father, Randhir had an older stepbrother, Hridya Rai about whom he had never heard. Shobha learnt that when Hridya Rai grew up he decided to go in search of his father; he left home and was not heard of for many years. Finally the family received one letter from Hridya several years later saying that he was in Iraq. Hridya's mother stayed on in Baijudhia village and was looked after by the family till she died in 1965. It was an unexpected twist in the family history.

Shobha made plans to visit India; she decided to go to Rishikesh to attend a one-month long teacher's training programme for yoga.

Shobha felt excited as well a bit nervous about the trip and meeting the relatives. So she did a bit of travelling, she went to Kolkata, Jaipur and Agra. It was meant to familiarise her with the country and prepare her to begin the visit to Gorakhpur and Baijudhia village. There was some sad news for Shobha just before she left Canada – Cousin Banwari Rai passed away a few days before she started her journey. He was the only relative she was familiar with through the long chats on the phone and his death made her a bit anxious about her trip.

As she drove down from Gorakhpur to Baijudhia village, Shobha's mind kept going back to her childhood days, to the stories her father and *fua* (father's sister) used to relate about life in India – stories they had heard from their parents. Anticipation and anxiety built up, Shobha said, "but the way my visit to the village turned out was much more than what I expected. I was very emotional, on several occasions I found myself choking up as I met the *parivaar* (families) of both of my grandfather's brothers."

At Baijudia village, Shobha heard the family story; it was a confirmation of some parts of the history she had heard before. The family tree was related to her – it told of Vasudev Rai of Baijudia village, who had three sons, Bhairon, Gopinath and Manohar. Bhairon was the eldest who had gone away to Fiji while Gopinath and Manohar stayed on at home, though Manohar's family moved to another village close by. Gopinath Rai had three sons, Bechan Rai, Vishwanath Rao and Bisessar Rai; Bechan Rai's son was Banwari Rai – Shobha's first contact with the Indian side of her family.

At Baijudhia village, Shobha was welcomed by the family of Gopinath Rai. Later in the afternoon, she left for Baijnathpur village, a village on the road to Gorakhpur town, where she met the descendants of Manohar Rai, the youngest of the three Rai brothers. Unlike other people of Indian origin meeting their relatives in the ancestral village, Shobha had no trouble in communicating with them since she spoke fluent Hindi.

There were five generations of the family present in the village, including to Shobha's great surprise, her *aja's* nephew, Manohar Rai's son. "I was taken by surprise when I met my grandfather's nephew, Shivmurthi Rai. I had not known about him, he is my Dad's first cousin. It was an emotional reunion. I was deeply moved at meeting him because I felt that I had a father figure still alive."

Going around the villages, meeting new relatives, seeing the places where her grandparents lived was "an exhilarating experience," Shobha recalled. "So many emotions were aroused by the different things that I saw and the people I met. I was startled to see one second cousin, Nagendra – he resembled my *aja*."

A strong confident woman herself, Shobha Rai was pleased to find that the women of her Indian family were strong-headed and independent minded. "I was surprised by one of the young girls of the family. She spoke fluent English and told me that she wanted to join the army and go to the NDA (National Defence Academy). There was a lively debate among all the women relatives who had gathered there about her joining the army, but she sounded so confident when she spoke about her ambitions." Shobha felt at home among her relatives and felt an immediate connection with them. They asked about her family in Canada and Fiji. The younger cousins exchanged phone numbers and email addresses with her and promised to get in touch with Shobha's brother in Fiji and invite him to visit his Indian home.

Note

1. *Tears in Paradise: A Personal and Historical Journey 1879-2004* by Rajendra Prasad, Glade Publishers, Auckland, 2004.

Stories from the Caribbean: Parmanand Singh, Ashwini Kumar, Sita, Vishnu Bisram

Roots seekers who have been successful in tracing their ancestors genealogy have often described it as a deeply emotional journey. Parmanand Singh, a pharmacist of Ontario, Canada began his own search for his family roots on the request of a relative, but Parmanand got more and more engrossed in the search and soon it became his own personal journey of discovery.

Parmanand Singh's uncle (father's youngest brother) Hamarine (Len) Singh was terminally ill in 2006 when he asked his nephew to research the family background. Len Singh explained that it had long been his dream to find out more about the family history and where they came from. Ever since he became ill, Len Singh had been thinking about his dream and he hoped someone in the family would take it forward, he said. It was a last request that was hard for Parmanand to ignore, and he eventually promised his uncle that he would do his best to fulfil his dream.

Len Singh gave Parmanand all the bits of information that he had collected about the family. Len had gathered that their ancestor, Punno Singh (also known as Mahabir) migrated to Dutch Guiana, now known as Suriname in 1913. He was about 18 years old at that time and the ship that he travelled on was called the Sutlej II. According to Len Singh, it was an impression among the family circle that Punno Singh's family had owned a school in the village in a place called Basti in India.

These few facts were all the information Parmanand had when he began his search. Since his grandfather, Punno Singh had initially migrated to Suriname, Parmanand's first point of call was to contact the Suriname government for information. He was advised to check their website called the Historic Database of Suriname and was sent the link to the site. Parmanand clicked on the link, went on the website and typed his grandfather's name.

To Parmanand's delight the name Punno Singh popped up with several details of his life. "The information that my uncle had given me was all there so I knew this was the person I was looking for. I was really excited at seeing my grandfather's name and so many details on the screen – the exact date he had arrived, the village he came from, and the estate he was contracted to work on – it was all there. Also I knew it was the right person because they had information about my grandmother. I cross checked my grandmother's information which listed the names of her first three children; they were the names of my eldest uncle and my two aunts who were born in Suriname. (My dad, Rambharose was Punno Singh's third son) this convinced me that all the details given were correct," Parmanand Singh explained.

Punno Singh and his wife, Nusia had seven sons and four daughters. From Suriname, the family moved to Guyana in 1921 or thereabouts and lived there till the time of Punno Singh's death in 1952. His children later migrated to Canada, America, Britain and Germany.

Punno Singh arrived in Paramaribo, Suriname on January 7, 1914. He lived there fulfilling his contract at the Waterloo plantation until January 7, 1919. "According to the records he married my grandmother in Nickerie, Suriname and it is unclear what year they moved to British Guiana. My grandmother, Nusia was born in Demerara, British Guiana and her family moved back to India – either to Benares or Calcutta and then went to Suriname in April 1912.Three of their children were born in Suriname and the rest in British Guiana. The family stayed in British Guiana where the kids and grandkids grew up and started immigrating to Canada, the US, England and Germany from the 1960s onwards.

Very few family members remain in Guyana now. Only one of Punno Singh's offspring is still alive; her name is Sursettie Persaud, she is in her 70s and she lives in Canada."

Parmanand had collected all this information but did not know how to proceed further in his search. The family made efforts to locate the village. Parmanand's cousin, Budhan Devi (called Devi) said: "It had always been a burning desire among the family to find out about our grandfather. He had cut off from his family in India and it had always bothered us that we did not know about our relatives there." The family in Guyana knew that Punno Singh had run away from home because his uncle, a teacher in the local school had beaten him. Punno and a friend decided to leave home together. They stowed away on a ship but were discovered when the ship docked in Mauritius. Punno was put to work as a checker boy – loading staples on the ship while his friend decided to return home. The ship sailed on to Suriname where he became an indentured worker for five years.

In Suriname, Punno Singh married 13-year old Nusia and had their first child a year later. After Punno Singh and Nusia had moved to British Guiana with their children, Punno wanted to go home to India. Punno was literate and used to write letters to his parents. His parents were keen that Punno return home but wanted him to come alone. Punno Singh had six children by that time and he did not want to leave his family behind. He decided not to return and stopped writing to his parents in India.

Another member of the family, Dr M Gopal was going to India on a tour. He tried to locate the family home in India during his trip. Dr Gopal went to Basti for a day and tried to locate the village but could not make any progress. It was a great disappointment for the family. It was some time after Dr Gopal's futile trip that Parmanand Singh met Ashwini Kumar Rajpal, an old friend and a member of the extended family. Parmanand related all the search efforts they had made and how they had reached a dead end.

Parmanand spoke about his strong motivation to go ahead with his search – it was no longer merely his uncle, Len's last request, it had become his own personal search for his ancestral history, he said.

Ashwini Kumar explained that he had some contacts in India who could help him pursue the search and locate his grandfather's village. Parmanand gave Ashwini Kumar all the search material he had collected about his grandparents. Ashwini Kumar's contacts began their research, and after some time, they were able locate the village. They were even able to find some members of the family who were still living in the village. Parmanand said. "Reading about the family and their place in history, it sure made us all proud to find out that they were involved in the First War of Independence of 1857. It also made us sad to find out that they were persecuted by the British from there on."

Parmanand Singh was not able to make plans to go to India, but his young cousin, Budhan Devi made the trip to India in September 2009 with a group of people who were travelling through India. Devi, an insurance consultant in New York was thrilled to be travelling with her mother, Radha and cousin Rajcoomarie to Rudhauli village. Devi explained: "It has always been a burning desire in our family to find out about our grandfather, he was estranged from his family. We did not know how to locate the ancestral village, but my cousin managed to obtain some information from the archives. Now we have finally got in touch with some distant relations in Rudhauli."

Ashwini Kumar had assigned the case of Punno Singh to a non-governmental organisation in Uttar Pradesh, the Sri Ramanand Saraswati Pustakalaya, (SRSP) located in Jokhera in Azamgarh district. The SRSP team began analysing the information they had about Punoo Singh; the fact that he was a *thakur* by caste and his family ran a school in Rudhouli (now spelt as Rudhauli) indicated that he belonged to a prominent family of the area. The team travelled to Basti and began their search.

The SRSP team started their search in Basti town with a visit to the office of the Deputy Inspector General (DIG) of Police. Research teams have on occasion run into rough weather while making inquires in a village, especially when they do not have accurate information about the person they are trying to locate. Search teams have been mistaken for revenue collectors or inspectors for the Below Poverty Line (BPL) schemes or other petty government officials. Taking the help and advice of senior police officials can open many doors as well as provide vital information.

The police official sent word to the officer in charge of the Rudhauli police post to assist the search team. Rudhauli bazar was now a bustling township with a population of about 10,000, it has several educational institutions. When the search team reached Rudhauli thana (police station), the police officer in charge said that since the family they were trying to trace was associated with a private school the team should focus on that aspect. He suggested that they meet one of the oldest residents of the township, Jagannath Prasad. Ninety-six-year old Jagannath Prasad was a retired school teacher; he said that Rudhauli used to have a teachers training college and an inter-college that was started earlier. But these had changed hands over the decades. He suggested that they talk to an old *thakur* family of Rudhauli and gave directions to their home.

In the absence of written records, search teams have to base their inquiries on conversations with a large number of people. As the link to education had not proved fruitful, the team tried to meet elders in the thakur community. The team was introduced to Krishna Pratap Singh, who recalled that his father, Munnu babu used to talk about someone named Mahabir who had run away from home. Mahabir was remembered because he belonged to the illustrious family of Shivgulam Singh. Shivgulam Singh was a freedom fighter who had fought against the British. He was killed in a battle near Paida Pokhare and his property was confiscated by the government, according to Krishna Pratap Singh. Punno Singh was also known as Mahabir, but there was little else to connect this Mahabir with Punno Singh.

The team returned to Basti and began the research anew from another angle. Since Punno Singh was a *thakur*, a land owning caste, his name should appear on the village land records. The team went to the District Record Room to look through the revenue records. However, the junior officials at the District Record Room were not helpful at all. They were reluctant to go through the dusty pile of ancient records and put off the team on one excuse or the other. The search team then sought the help of their contact in the police, who persuaded the junior revenue officials to take out the old records. They also helped to locate an Urdu translator, Syed Munshi, who was familiar with the language in which the old records were written.

The '*fasli bandobast*' or land revenue records were started during the Mughal period when the revenue was assessed on the basis of the harvest or '*fasal*' produced in a single season. Syed Munshi read through each page of the *fasli bandobast* for Rudhauli village. In the *fasli* records, Syed Munshi found the name of one Daulat Singh, who had three sons – Shivgulam Singh, Shivbaksh Singh and Jeet Singh. A painstaking search through the revenue record for three decades showed up the name Punnu in the record. The record carried the names of Daulat Singh's grandsons – Budhu Singh, son of Shivbaksh Singh and Punnu Singh, son of Jeet Singh.

The search team's efforts had been successful – Punnu Singh or Punno Singh was the son of Jeet Singh. The land record also connected Punno Singh and his father, Jeet Singh with the patriotic martyr, Shivgulam as Jeet Singh was the youngest brother of Shivgulam. Krishna Pratap Singh's story was proved correct! The search team got photocopies made of the revenue record and then began the next part of their search – to locate members of the family living in Rudhauli.

The search team reached Rudhauli to meet the descendents of Shivgulam Singh and his brothers. They were directed to meet Urmila Singh at the Rudhauli Junior High School. Urmila Singh explained that Shivgulam Singh was her grandfather's grandfather. According to Urmila Singh, Shivgulam Singh was the '*gujaaredar*' – the representative of Bansi State for collecting taxes (*lagan*) from 156 villages in the area. He rose in revolt against the British and died fighting the British forces during the Uprising of 1857.

The family's fortunes declined after the death of Shivgulam Singh. The British sought to arrest the rest of the family, who dispersed to different places to evade detention. Much of the family land and its assets were confiscated at that time. Later, some of the family members returned to Rudhauli to live off the small bit of land still left in their possession.

The family staying in Rudhauli were the descendents of Shivgulam Singh's brother, Shivbaksh Singh and his son, Budhu Singh. Budhu Singh's grandson's three daughters, Savitri, Urmila and Gayatri and their families lived in Rudhauli in a house that is next door to the Dileshwari Inter College. But Urmila said that they had no connection with the Inter College any longer though it had once belonged to their family many decades ago. All three sisters taught at government schools in the area.

A local historian, Ravi Pratap Singh related the story of Shivgulam Singh. Shivgulam Singh was a zamindar of Radhauli; he died at Paida Pokhare, some 18 kms off the Basti-Bansi road, after giving a tough fight to the British. He is a folk hero in the region and folk songs have been written about his bravery. A pillar commemorating his battle was erected at Paida Pokhare and a fair is held there on November 25th every year. Ravi Pratap Singh pointed to a large mound behind the Dileshwari Inter College and said that it was the site of a huge *haveli* (mansion) that belonged to Shivgulam Singh. The British had demolished the *haveli* after the arrest of Shivgulam

Singh; this was one of the penalties meted out to freedom fighter families by the British after the 1857 War of Independence.

According to Parmanand Singh, "The members of the family were interested in pursuing this history. They were quite pleasantly surprised at the outcome of this search and to see the results of history and the family history. Some of my cousins, Devi and Radha have made the trip and so has my sister Rajcoomarie, and met the cousins still living in Rudhauli. All of them were touched by the closeness they felt at meeting the cousins even after one century of a missing link."

The search for Punno Singh's family history took some twists and turns, but the oral history related by Urmila corroborated the evidence of the land records. A year later, Devi and her mother, Radha visited Radhauli and met Urmila and her sisters bringing the estranged sections of the family together. Devi said: "I can't express how I felt at home. I can't speak the language, but I didn't feel like a foreigner. I felt a connection with my cousins and felt that it is part of me."

Ashwini Kumar Rajapal is associated with a non-governmental organisation, International Foundation for Vedic Science and has been instrumental in discovering the ancestral histories of several persons of Indian origin. His interest in the subject stemmed from his own search and travels through India following the path of the *jahajees* (shipmates as the indentured workers called themselves). Ashwini Kumar had tried to obtain copies of emigration passes for his great grandparents from the National Archives of Guyana.

Ashwini Kumar wrote about his experiences during a visit to Calcutta (now Kolkata) when his hosts took him to a tour of the area that was a departure point for the *girmitiyas*. "The quarantine area across the street is now a new government building. This is within walking distance of Eden Gardens – the largest cricket stadium in the world. We then drove by the Shiv Mandir – one of the few places *girmitiyas* were allowed to visit. Unfortunately, the temple was engulfed by commercial establishments and does not have the look of a place of worship."

It was when Ashwini Kumar Rajpal returned from this trip to India that he received the three emigration passes of his ancestors from Guyana. One of the passes gave an address in Jaipur district; it was the emigration pass of Rajpal's great-grandfather, his dad's maternal grandfather. Ashwini Kumar sent off this information to a person whom he had met during his recent travels, and who lived in Jaipur. A couple of weeks later his friend replied to say that the area was now in Dausa district after the last reconfiguration of districts. He had despatched copies of the emigration passes to another friend, Dr Arya so that he could make some inquires. Dr Arya got in touch with an acquaintance who worked in a Jaipur newspaper, who in turn contacted his colleague based in Dausa.

A few months later, Ashwini Kumar Rajpal was invited to attend a wedding in Panchkula near Chandigarh in India. He thought it would be a good opportunity to attend the wedding and also try to trace his roots. In Delhi, he met an official working with the India Tourism office, Anil Oraw who had got interested in the story of the descendents of *girmitiyas* when he had helped some Indo-Fijians to trace their roots. He had been posted in Australia at that time. He sent emails to his colleagues in Jaipur and Calcutta to ask them to help Ashwini Kumar when he reached those cities.

In Jaipur, Ashwini Kumar hired an interpreter, who could translate from Rajasthani to English and then boarded a bus to Dausa. They made some inquires in Dausa and learnt that Manpur, the village named in his *par-nani's* (great-grandmother's) emigration pass was not too far away. They hired an auto-rickshaw to go to Chandera, his great-grandfather's village.

At Chandera, Ashwini Kumar Rajpal and his guide-interpreter spoke to some villagers but no one had heard of his *nana's* family. A couple of the older villagers promised to make some inquires in the neighbourhood later in the evening when people came back from their farms. Ashwini Kumar and his escort checked into motel in a nearby town for the night so that they could continue with their search the next day. Late that evening, one of the villagers rang up to say that they had made no progress.

By early next morning, the situation had changed. The local village official called on the phone to say that he had information on *Nana's* family. Ashwini Kumar and the guide rushed over to the official's house – he was waiting for them eagerly. They saw that a goodly crowd had gathered at the house. The official showed them that he had already drawn out a family tree in Hindi with *nana's* name. Since Ashwini Kumar did not follow Hindi, the official switched to broken English and began pointing out some of Rajpal's relatives in the crowd.

It was a totally unexpected encounter and Ashwini Kumar was lost for words at this sudden development. He related his feelings at this surprising encounter: "It was a complete surprise as I did not expect to meet the relatives so quickly. I was also overwhelmed with the attention as it seemed the whole village had showed up by then. After a while we were taken to *nana's* ancestral home which is now abandoned. We then proceeded to the home of two of *nana's* brother's grandchildren and their families. Here I learned that the family had assumed that *nana* had become a *sadhu* (ascetic) and had gone away up the Himalayas. They never knew he had immigrated to British Guiana. I was interviewed by a reporter from the Rajasthan Patrika, it had been arranged by the village official. The family asked me to plant a *Neem* tree in honour of my visit and the rejoining of our families."

The discovery of their relatives in Rajasthan had a special significance for Ashwini Kumar Rajpal and his parents for he had lived with his *nana* as a young child. There was great excitement in the village and Ashwini Kumar was given a tour of the village, shown the school and the library before they were escorted to their bus for Jaipur. It was a most satisfying day for Ashwini Kumar, the discovery of his *nana's* house and a bunch of relatives who welcomed him warmly into their homes and rejoiced in the meeting of distant relatives.

From Rajasthan, Ashwini Kumar began another momentous journey to Varanasi in Uttar Pradesh. At Varanasi station, Deepak Kumar who had located Ashwini Kumar's father's grandfather's *(aja)* village was waiting for him. His ancestral village was Jaitpore but Deepak Kumar had discovered that the family had since moved to Bhagwanpur village, some distance from Jaitpore. The next morning the two of them left for Bhagwanpur village. On reaching Bhagwanpur, Ashwini Kumar was taken to meet an old man called Buddhu Mallah. Some people sitting with Buddhu Mallah claimed that he was approximately 110 years old. Ashwini Kumar was surprised to learn that Buddhu Mallah was his father's cousin.

Ashwini Kumar related: "Buddhu Mallah's children, grandchildren and great-grandchildren totaling approximately 60 persons, live in a few houses next to each other; therefore it was easy to meet them. We were taken to the outskirts of the village, there was a river flowing by the village and a mountain range just beyond the river. It was very scenic. I was told by some members of the family that they would be moving to another village since there are no properties left to buy in this village."

Ashwini Kumar was then taken to his *aja's* ancestral village – Jaitpore – it was located at the base of the mountain. He was told by his relatives that the villagers had been forced to move by the landlords who wanted the land for themselves. It is only lately that some families had started moving back. It was these people who had returned to Jaitpore who had eventually led the researcher, Deepak Kumar to Buddhu Mallah.

That evening Ashwini Kumar and his guide took a train to Gaya where they stayed in a small hotel near the railway station. Early next morning they went out in search of the *panda* – a priest who acts as the record keeper and maintains the family history of a particular area – this was the *panda* for the Bhagwanpur/Jaitpore area. But the *panda* could not find any entries in his records for Ashwini Kumar's *aja's* family. It was a little disappointing after the excitement and emotion of yesterday's meeting with relatives; he would have liked to add his family's name to the family *pothi* (record book) to make a complete family tree. But then Ashwini Kumar was undaunted as he had other searches to complete.

Ashwini Kumar's grandmother, Shewbarti had travelled to British Guiana as a young child in 1895 accompanying her 22-year old mother, Gangaia. Gangaia's family was a land owning family and some members of Gangaia's family who remained in the old village were still working the land. Ashwini Kumar recalled that his grandmother, Shewbarti was heartbroken when he left to make his home in Canada. It was perhaps the second time in her lifetime that she had seen dislocation of the family.

Kumar was able to draw satisfaction from being able to meet relatives from his great-grandmother and great-grandfather's side of the family in the last few days. These meetings enthused Ashwini Kumar Rajpal to get more actively involved in the process of tracing the roots, for himself and for others. He took up the searches for other people who asked him for help after hearing of his successes. And not very long time later, the contacts that Ashwini Kumar had built up so painstakingly in different parts of India were able to locate the whereabouts of his wife's ancestral home.

Just as Ashwini Kumar was searching for his ancestral heritage in India, his wife, Sita was trying to trace the village from where her ancestor had begun his journey to British Guiana in 1899. Sita's ancestor, her great-grandfather (her maternal grandmother's father) was named Chutkan. The family had their grandmother's (*nani's*) birth certificate. The birth certificate gave *nani's* father's name and other details that helped them trace Chutkan's emigration pass from the Guyanese records. According to the emigration pass, Chutkan's village was called Gohna in the district of Basti. The search began from Basti town for Chutkan, son of

Gunga of village Gohna in the jurisdiction of Bansi thana (police station). Chutkan's caste was listed as '*looh*' caste and his next of kin was given as his brother, Gohre.

The researchers had very little information to go on except the name and village of the migrant. The search team decided to begin their quest at the District Record Room in Basti. The land revenue records are usually a good place to start especially if the date of departure is known, for it sets a cut-off point for looking through the records. Chutkan had reached British Guiana in 1899 and records prior to that year had to be examined.

Fortunately for the researchers they met a local advocate, Vijaysen Singh at the Basti district court who was well versed in local affairs. He told them that the district had been bifurcated and Bansi thana had been transferred to the new district of Siddhartha Nagar. Siddhartha Nagar district had been carved out of Basti district in 1988 during the process of reorganisation of the larger districts. Bansi was a small township that was located at a distance of 47 kms from Basti town.

Vijaysen Singh had become quite interested in the search project; he was fascinated by the story of Indians who were taken away from their native place to a foreign country and whose descendants were seeking to reconnect with their relatives. He became a good source of information for the researchers. Singh had another valuable piece of advice to offer. According to Vijaysen Singh, Chutkan was most likely to have been from the *Lodh* caste; *Looh* caste was probably a misspelling as there was no such caste in the region. The search team consulted other people in Basti town who also supported Vijaysen Singh's view that that Chutkan's caste would be Lodh caste.

The search team continued to look through the revenue records but despite long effort could not find any reference to Chutkan or his father Gunga or his brother Gohre in the old documents. It was Vijaysen Singh, who pointed out that it was highly unlikely that Gunga or Chutkan's name would appear in the land records as the *Lodh* community did not own any land in those days. The revenue records list the names of the owners or those who had taken the land on lease or those who paid the *lagan* (land revenue). *Lodhs* were not a land owning community in the old days though many of them now own land in the rural areas.

The search team then decided to direct their research in Bansi town to look for Gohna village. On reaching Bansi, the team went to the police station where they met the Inspector-in-charge. The Inspector explained to them that there was no village known as Gohna under the limits of Bansi thana, but there were two villages with the name Gonha Deeh and Gonha Taal. He also told them that Gonha Taal did not have any Lodh residents, but Gonha Deeh had a large *Lodh* community.

The search team then went on to Gonha Deeh. They were accompanied by a police constable, who took them to meet some of the older folk in the village. Seventy-year-old Awatar listened to the search team and then told them a story that had been told her by her mother-in-law, Ghurna. Ghurna had said that three men from the village had gone to the *zamindar's* (local landowner) house to ask for some '*koda*' – a local coarse grain and they never returned home. The story implies that it was a time of scarcity when men had to ask for coarse grain.

As a crowd gathered around the team members, more people joined in the conversation. One man called Dayaram Lodh recalled that his father, Ramasre Lodh, had sometimes talked about Gareeb's uncle, Chutkan who had had gone '*pardesh*' (abroad). Then Lakhpat, son of Sohrat said that several letters from some foreign place had arrived addressed to his father. The last letter had come in 1986. However, Lakhpat did not possess any of the letters. He had taken the letters to the post office to have the address written on an envelope, and had left them behind by mistake. When he went back to get the old letters they could not be found.

An elderly woman, Isra, wife of Lochan, said that her father, Gelhai used to relate that Gareeb's chacha went to Demra Island. Gareeb's father's name was Gobre, she said. Chutkan's father's name was Gunga and his next of kin, his brother, was listed as Gohare. It is likely that Gobre was taken down as Gohare in the colonial records. In the early years of migration to British Guinea, the country was known as Demerara, a province of British Guinea. In India the name could have been known as Demra, just as Mauritius became Mirich desh and Australia was known as Telia by Punjabi villagers.

The researchers were directed to meet Rajaram, son of Bhagwanta and Ashrafi Lodh. Rajaram's mother, Bhagwanta was Gobre's granddaughter; daughter of his son, Kalpu. They learnt that Gobre had two other sons, Gareeb and Jeete. While Jeete did not marry, Gareeb had two daughters who were married in distant villages. Rajaram and his son, Gangaram lived in the old family home in Gohna Deeh.

When Sita and Ashwini Kumar came visiting Gohna Deeh in September 2009, they had got delayed in reaching the village. It was evening when they Gohna Deeh, and Rajaram was away working in the fields. The family had one bigha of farm land and workers were planting garlic in the field. Sita and Ashwini Kumar could not meet Rajaram for it was getting dark and they had to return to town as they had been advised not to travel during the night. But it was a homecoming for Sita; her cousin, Rajaram's wife was overwhelmed with joy at meeting her. The family could not work out how they should welcome these prosperous visitors from a foreign country. Finally, Chandrawati, Rajaram's wife greeted them in a traditional ritual at the front door of the house with a palm full of sugar and a *lota* (urn) of water; she then ushered them into the family home.

"Chandrawati could not do enough to make us comfortable," Ashwini Kumar said. Gangaram and his wife hovered around them but they "were a bit shy and did not say much," he added. Sita inquired about the members of the family, she wanted to know the kind of education the young ones were getting in the village. The young children of the locality had gathered around, gazing at the foreign visitors. Ashwini and Sita took photographs with Chandrawati and other members of the family and with the village children. Soon it was time to bid goodbye to the new found relatives. The meeting was too short, but the links had been reconnected between the families.

Tracing roots has become important to a large number of Indo-Caribbean people and more and more of them have been travelling to India to find relatives or at least visit the village where their great-grand parents came from. Vishnu Bisram, an educator and newspaper columnist of Guyana felt it was important to trace one's family roots to understand from whence one came and how one's ancestors lived as well as what were the conditions that motivated them to emigrate to the Caribbean and elsewhere.

Bisram said: "A longing and deep burning desire pushed me to find my cousins in India. I went to great lengths to trace my roots and I am happy to have found them. My interest in finding my ancestors was fuelled by a burning desire to learn more about my background. My mother told me during a trip to India of how her grandparents were brought to then British Guiana in the 1890s. My mother revealed a lot about her grandparents as told by her grandmother; they came from 'princely family' and were kidnapped and brought aboard the ship for the lengthy journey to Guiana. While moving around in India, the scenes of village life reminded her of what her grandmother told her about the homes and way of life of the villagers. It was then and there I decided that I would make an earnest effort to trace my ancestral link to Mother India – to investigate where my ancestors came from and to find my distant relatives. I was successful in finding my paternal relatives while the search for my maternal relatives is ongoing."

When Vishnu Bisram began a search for the Emigrant Pass of his ancestors, he had virtually no information about them since his mother and other relatives did not know the names of their grand parents. Bisram explained that he did some backtracking to find his ancestors' ship documents, "From my mother's birth certificate, I was able to find the names of my grand parents. And from the grand parents' records, I was able to find their parents (my great-grand parents) names and when they came to Guiana. Having found their correct names as recorded on the ship's master list, I was able to obtain copies of their emigration passes."

According to Vishnu Bisram, the emigration pass is kept in the archives or at the General Post Office. Obtaining a copy of the pass was quite difficult, he said. It was a very lengthy, time consuming and costly process to obtain the documents and required a lot of patience and knowledge on how to find the document. Since the search can be done only someone who is employed within the office and since the workers may have other requests, the process takes a long time, he said.

The immigrant's documents are not in good condition; they are falling apart. Because of the advanced stage of deterioration (faded writing, broken pieces of the paper, etc.) of some of the passes, it was not an easy task to decipher the information on them. They are written in old English calligraphic style making them difficult to read. The photocopies were not clear and there was difficulty in figuring out the name of the village. Bisram showed the document to several handwriting specialists and after some effort came to a conclusion on the name of the sub-district and village.

Ghurbatore (great-grandfather) and Amru (his wife) came to British Guiana on the same ship and were bounded to the same estate. It is not known if they knew each other prior to boarding the ship as they were from different districts separated by over a hundred miles. They got married in Guiana and had five children; Vishnu Bisram's *aja* (grandfather) was their oldest son.

Bisram managed to find the emigration passes for his paternal grand parents as well. He sent the documents to a contact in India who had earlier helped to locate the ancestral homes of his cousins in Guyana. The contact went through post office records, land titles and spoke to elderly people and luckily managed to locate Bisram's great-grandfather and greatgrandmother's villages in two districts not far from the city of Varanasi. Vishnu Bisram's own research in the indenture migration had shown that tens of thousands of immigrants had come to the Caribbean from the same area of eastern Uttar Pradesh on the border of Bihar. He travelled to his paternal great-grandparent's ancestral village and met some relatives but did not succeed in locating his maternal ancestral village.

"My maternal great-grandfather and great-grandmother were some kind of landlords and lived in a wealthy home which had servants to tend to their needs. They were kidnapped during a *teerat* (pilgrimage) and brought to Guiana against their will. It sounds like a fairy tale and I am determined to confirm the story as told to my mom by her *nani.*"

Bisram recalled that it was "an intensely emotional experience meeting my ancestral relatives during the two times I met with them in Azamgarh and Ghazipur. Amru was from Azamgarh District, Ranapur sub-district or thana, and village Jokhapur. Ghurbatore belonged to Ghazipur district, Kusmi village. Azamgarh and Ghazipur are about an hour apart by fast moving car. My ancestors were from poor villages with dirt roads not different from the old plantations of Guiana."

Bisram visited the two villages during a trip to India in February 2007. "I met one family in the morning and the other family in the evening. I did not spend much time with either relatives because of limited time at my hands. It was a very emotional welcome, quite unexpected. You have to actually experience it to know it," he said.

"The first encounter was an inspirational experience. It was filled with emotion with warm embraces and bowing to my feet by the younger ones and me to the older ones. The males lifted me up. There were singing and chanting. I was thrilled and they were overjoyed with tears; one lady cried inconsolably for over five minutes. I was led into their poor homes and offered tea. They were humble, loving and caring. They massaged my legs and feet. They took me around the yard and the little temple where they prayed and I offered prayers thanking the lord for finding them. I spoke with them with my broken Hindi and through a translator. They spoke with me in Hindi and we understood each other. They knew the relationship as told to them.

"Both sides of the family were quite excited to meet with me. A curious crowd of literally hundreds of people came to greet me when they saw a car enter into the area between the two separate villages; the two families don't know each other and I did not introduce them to one another. There were a lot of tears when we met and they were overjoyed to have found me. I was also driven with emotions, happy to find them. In searching for my relatives, there was a mixture of anticipation and sorrow in my heart. It was an experience that cannot be described but only felt.

"It saddens me that I did not trace my roots much sooner when my father and uncles were alive. It would have been nice for my father to have met his cousin. It would have been something my father would have appreciated. I am sure my late uncles would have been overjoyed to know about their distant cousins in Bharat. I stay in touch with my great grandmother's relatives phoning them on their cell phones. The relatives from my great grandfather's side do not speak English and it has been difficult staying in touch with them."

Like others who have been through the experience of meeting long lost relatives in the ancestral homeland, Vishnu Bisram also urged other *pravasi* Indians to search for their roots. "Stories told by our parents about their parents and grandparents should be written down and treasured for future generations or they will be lost forever. I regret I did not pen mine down. I urge everyone to do so. To get started looking for your family tree, start with your mom and dad if you don't have information on your grandparents like me. Talk to aunts and uncles. You'll be surprised how many people love to talk about their parents' past," according to Vishnu Bisram.

Conclusion: Search Facilities in India

Family searches are getting easier in India as travel in the rural hinterland has become more convenient. The road network in the rural areas has been expanded, most villages can be reached by road and vehicles can be hired to take the visitor to the smaller villages off the main highways. Some amount of preliminary search can be conducted on the internet through the number of websites that give information on Indian districts. Tech-savvy overseas Indians have been able to collect a good deal of information from the internet, bringing them closer to locating the ancestral home through their own efforts.

The case of Faizal Dulull of Mauritius is an example of how much can be learnt through the internet. Dulull obtained a copy of the emigration pass of his great-great-grandfather, who migrated in June 1858 from the archives. The village address was Nurunjenpore, Zillah Arrah, Pergunnah Bhojepora. But Bhojepora had been sub-divided several times in the past 150 years; the village could be in any of five present-day districts. Dullul surfed the internet and scrolled through several websites on Bihar to glean whatever information he could get regarding his search. On www.brandbihar.com he found a list of districts, blocks and villages. He discovered five villages of the name of Nurunjenpore, now spelled Niranjanpur, in the three districts of Rohtas, Buxar and Kaimur on the site.

Dulull then searched through the list of voters on the Bihar State Election Commission for the name Sah, for his ancestor's father's name had been written down as Lollsah in the emigration record. He could locate several people with the family name of

Sah in three of the villages named Niranjanpur. Locating the Niranjanpur from where his ancestor began his journey to Mauritius would entail travelling to each village to identify the 'real' Niranjanpur. That is still a work in process.

There are government agencies and a few private agencies that have developed some amount of expertise in searching for ancestral villages based on the information given in the Emigration Passes. The Indian government's Ministry of Overseas Indian Affairs set up a Trace Your Roots Programme as part of its diaspora outreach programme. The Ministry signed a memorandum of understanding with a professional roots searcher, Chandrasekhar Tiwary of Indiroots for carrying out the ancestral searches. Tiwary had been an independent genealogist for over ten years before he entered into the arrangement with the Ministry of Overseas Indian Affairs. During this period he had investigated over a hundred search requests.

The Ministry of Overseas Indian Affairs official website has a form for roots seekers to fill in giving all the relevant information that is available with them. After filling in the form, the roots seekers are required to deposit the form at the Indian embassy or consulate in the country where they reside with a fee of ₹ 20,000 or its equivalent in foreign currency. Under the terms of the contract , the Ministry pays ₹ 6,000 to to the researcher to begin the search for the applicant's ancestral home village. Depending on the kind of details the roots seeker provides, the searcher is expected to prepare a family tree, document the whereabouts of the family home and identify close surviving relatives within a period of three months.

This information is sent to the applicant for confirmation of its genuineness. In case the search has been successful, the Ministry pays the searcher an additional ₹ 14,000 for its services. However, if the search is unsuccessful the searcher is paid a sum of ₹ 4,000 for its expenses and ₹ 10,000 is refunded to the applicant. In case the roots seekers wish to travel to India and visit the family home, they can use the information provided to them to organise their tour with the help of an accredited travel agency.

State governments such as the Uttar Pradesh government, Bihar state government, government of Goa have their own ancestral search programmes. The Rajasthan government is also in the process of setting up a roots search programme for the thousands of Rajasthanis living around the world. Other states like Gujarat have their own outreach programmes for reaching out to their diaspora.

The Uttar Pradesh government launched its 'Discover Your Roots' scheme in 2006.Under the programme, the Uttar Pradesh Tourism department undertakes to locate the birth place of the roots seeker's ancestor based on information available from emigration passes, old letters, school certificates, passports, land records, records in religious places (*pothis*), personal inquires and local legends. The department also makes all arrangements for people who want to visit the homes of their forefathers. The Tourism department carries out the ancestral search at a fee of US $150, and in the event that the search is unsuccessful, the department refunds $75 to the roots seeker. The UP government's Discover Your Roots programme is applicable only to those roots seekers whose ancestors were residents of the state of Uttar Pradesh.

The Discover Your Roots website receives up to three to four queries each month about ancestral searches. The project office has two teams of researchers who travel out to the district of the migrant and spend three to four days carrying out a search by checking official records, visiting the villages and talking to the village elders. The team usually makes two trips to the ancestral village to confirm the oral history and locate any living relatives.

In case of a successful search the Uttar Pradesh tourism department offers to make tour arrangements at a reasonable cost for the family history seeker to travel to his or her ancestral village. The Tourism Department sends out an escort and guide with the visitor and also arranges a small traditional welcome function for the visitor at the village. The escort/guide proves useful for interpreting the villagers' dialect and explaining local customs to the foreign visitor.

A few years ago the Uttar Pradesh roots programme took up a pilot project in Ballia district. Ballia is a district which had a high rate of outward migration during the indenture period. The government appointed field supervisors for the project who stayed in Ballia and visited the villages in the district. While visiting a particular village the field supervisor met the *Lekhpal* (village official), the *gram pradhan* (village head) and the senior citizens in the village to collect information and oral history of the village. The searchers also collected the local songs and ballads to check whether there was any reference to persons who had left the village and gone away to distant places. The supervisors found information of 56 residents of Ballia district who had left for Trinidad as indentured workers. It has also taken up a project to locate the emigration passes of indentured workers in the State Archives and digitise the land records in the districts from where a large number of migrants went overseas as indentured workers.

The Bihar government started its own Trace Your Roots programme in 2008. Prime Minister of Mauritius, Navin Ramgoolam's visit to his ancestral village had generated a wave of excitement among the overseas Indians who were keen on tracing their own roots. The Bihar government's programme got a large number of requests from potential roots seekers; almost a hundred queries came in within a period of two years. The majority of the requests were from Mauritius. People wrote to the Indian High Commission in Mauritius, many wrote to the Mauritius High Commission in New Delhi, while others wrote directly to the Bihar government. These queries were sent to the Bihar government, which handed them over to the state Culture department for processing. Some of the queries with sufficient leads to the original village were successfully traced.

The roots search program was later assigned to the Bihar Foundation, an autonomous organisation of the Bihar state government. The Bihar Foundation has a form on its website for people who want to initiate a search in Bihar. The Bihar Foundation is in the process of working out a strategy to involve local not-for-profit, non-governmental organisations in the region to locate the ancestral villages and organise a roots seeker's tour of the area with a local flavour. The desire to connect with the old homeland is so strong that many family searchers who are not able to find their family homes are still keen to visit India and tour the region which has prominently figured in the oral narrative of the family.

Searching through the old land records in Bihar poses some difficulties as the land records and revenue records are written in *Kaithi* script and there is a shortage of people who are fluent in reading and translating *Kaithi* into Bhojpuri or Hindi. The other difficulty lies in the emigration pass itself, where information is incorrectly written down. A search request received in 2009 gave the address as village Rampur, thana Behar, district Patna. The initial search in Patna district was unsuccessful. The search team went through the old administrative records and decided to take a chance that Behar could refer to Biharsharif which had been part of Patna district at one time. It proved to be the right decision for they located Rampur village. But this was a rare case since it is near impossible to locate an ancestral village if the information given on the emigration pass is incorrect.

The state government of Goa has begun a programme to Know Goa; it provides a tour of Goa and its historical places for young people of Goan origin. It also provides some assistance for overseas Goans to search for their ancestors in Goa. Nostalgia is driving many people of Goan descent to search for their roots. Fortunately, the archives and the various kinds of records are in much better state of preservation in Goa compared to the rest of the country. Colonial era records are fairly well preserved as are church baptismal records. The village system and the rural clan networks have helped preserve the history of the region.

There are some private groups that undertake the ancestral searches in different areas. An Azamgarh based not-for profit organisation, Sri Ramanand Saraswati Pustakalya (SRSP) has been conducting roots searches in collaboration with Ashwini Kumar Rajpal of the International Foundation for Vedic Studies. It successfully completed ten roots searches in the first round of investigations and is currently working on another eight cases. The SRSP charges about ₹ 20,000 for carrying out a roots search, which usually involves two to three visits to a village to confirm that it is the genuine article.

The SRSP is based in Jokehara village of Azamgarh district and is involved in gender empowerment and imparting vocational training to youth and women of the area. Its workers were familiar with the region. They have visited small towns, looked at land records and spoken to the elderly men and women in the villages to identify the places from where people had migrated more than a hundred years ago.

The Antar Rashtiya Sahyog Parishad took up the trace your roots programme as far back as the 1980s. Several *pravasi* Indians had their ancestral villages located by the ARSP, which has local chapters in many of the towns of UP and Bihar. ARSP's main focus has been on improving ties with the Indian diaspora for more than two decades; ancestral searches were a service the NGO provided to overseas Indians who were keen to trace their ancestral roots. The searches were undertaken on the personal requests of individual *pravasi* Indians and were carried out by ARSP members.

Overseas Indians have also hired the services of private detectives to locate their ancestral village and any surviving relatives. Travel agencies too have carried out similar searches in a few instances. Dr Kamlesh Sharma of Australia was fortunate in locating a travel agent who took personal interest in searching out the ancestral family. Dr Sharma got in touch with Anishwar Singh through the Bhojpuri speaking network and Bhojpuriexpress.com website. Sharma consulted Anishwar Singh and Rakesh Mohan Singh on how to locate his great-grandfather's village. As a travel agent and tour operator, Anishwar Singh was quite used to the unfamiliar and out of the way destinations that some of his clients wanted to go to, but Dr Sharma's request was a new one for him.

Anishwar Singh was surprised when Dr Sharma spoke to him in Bhojpuri; he was intrigued by the foreigner who spoke chaste, but old fashioned Bhojpuri. Fiji baat, as the Hindi spoken in Fiji is called, is heavily based on Bhojpuri with a smattering of Brajbhasha and Awadhi mixed in it. Anishwar Singh was fascinated with the idea of seeking out an ancestral connection and got personally involved in Dr Sharma's search for a village in Basti district.

The information Anishwar Singh received from his friend was that the village was most likely to be near Basti town. Anishwar Singh drew up an itinerary for Dr Sharma to visit places Basti and other places associated with the indenture migration. It was a thoroughly enjoyable trip for Dr Sharma, who had done a good deal of research and reading about the region before he set out on his journey.

A strong sense of empathy built up between the Singhs and Dr Sharma during the search process, and the Singhs invited him to visit their village. Dr Sharma went to the Singhs village and stayed with their relatives for a couple of days. Kamlesh Sharma wrote about his experiences in India on his website and then authored a book on the subject. Sharma strongly recommended the tour agency BKS & DKS for bharatkisair.com and dunyakisair.com websites. In the next couple of years the Singhs received three more requests for searching ancestral villages in eastern Uttar Pradesh from overseas Indians who had read Dr Kamlesh Sharma's story.

The Singhs used their network of friends and relatives in the region to check out the facts. Though it entailed additional expense and effort the Singhs kept the cost of the search and the tour reasonable. "These requests came through Dr Sharmaji so we took them up. It was not for profit, we did the searches out of our own interest," said Rakesh Mohan. They even received requests to carry out searches in Tamil Nadu, Gujarat and Andhra Pradesh because of Dr Sharma's glowing testimonial for the Singhs efforts. In a couple of cases, they discovered the general location of the villages and the searchers made their own arrangements for travelling to the place.

In Mumbai and Kolkata, there are a few other travel agents and tour operators who have undertaken ancestral searches. In Kolkata, Calcutta Walks, an enterprise that organises walking tours of Kolkata has a steady stream of visitors who want to go to old places in the city that had warm associations with the memories of their ancestors. Calcutta had a large European population during the period when it was the main commercial and administrative centre during colonial days. It has several Scottish, Armenian, Jewish, Greek and even Chinese burial grounds that hold memories for their descendants.

There has been a revival of interest in the history and ethnic identity of the Anglo-Indian community in the past decade. Children of Anglo-Indians who had migrated to Australia and other parts of the world have been returning to Kolkata to look up the old home and the places they have heard of in the stories related by their parents and grandparents. Calcutta Walks provides special tours with the offer – 'Approach us with some basic information regarding your ancestry, and we shall work towards tracing the graves, if they're still intact, or at least find as much as possible about the individual and his Calcutta connection.' This is not limited to just finding the grave but goes onto mentally recreating the life and the times of the departed soul. According to Iftekhar

Ahsan of Calcutta Walks, some visitors have asked to be shown the areas associated with the indenture migration in Calcutta.

The Christian Burial Board which runs the four main cemeteries in Kolkata has begun the process of digitising the burial records for the period 1776 to 1911. The cemeteries have almost 20 visitors a day during the tourist season – all of them seeking to locate the graves of their ancestors. Many of the roots seekers also travel to the old railway towns and the cantonments to visit the cemeteries and the prominent landmarks they have heard about from their older relatives.

For Europeans searching for their ancestors' history, the British Association for Cemeteries in South Asia (BACSA) website has an archive that records about 1300 cemeteries with some inscriptions and photographs. Individual roots seekers who have searched for family roots and memorials of ancestors, have also created web sites that provide information of cemeteries or list names of Europeans in India from military records and church records. Some people have listed on their websites the headstone inscriptions and attached photographs of graves in specific cemeteries they have visited.

The Himachal Pradesh state government has brought out a book on the British colonial era cemeteries and churches in the state. The book: "Churches and Christian Cemeteries of Himachal Pradesh" gives a detailed history of the Christian cemeteries in the state where Europeans had been buried since 1829. It also lists the memorials that were erected in the memory of prominent British officials. The old hill towns of Shimla, Dharamshala, Kasauli, Dalhousie, Dharampur, Dagshai and Subathu still draw visitors from the UK and other parts of the world in search of places that are associated with their ancestors.

Unfortunately for the ancestral searches associated with the indenture period, as times goes by, it is becoming more and more difficult to locate the home villages. The old memories have faded and there are fewer old timers who would remember tales of the men and women who migrated to distant places. The older generation is dying out and most researchers complain that it is getting exceedingly difficult to verify the authenticity of a roots search. In earlier times, people rarely left the village, so any departure was an unusual event and was recalled and discussed for many years, even decades. Even when villages are identified, it is difficult to locate relatives because of the large scale migration that is taking place in the rural areas in India.

Nagendra, the lead ancestral searcher of the SRSP said that the ancestral searches were getting more and more difficult. "Most of the people who left their homes were poor, they did not own land and so were not listed in the revenue records. We have to rely on the memories of the old people, but they are dying out. The old stories are dying out with them. The younger generation in the villages are no longer interested in the old things or old events." The ancestral villages can be located if there is a correct address, but it has become difficult to verify the authenticity of the search. Roots seekers want some form of confirmation that it is their ancestor's own village, he explained.

Researchers contend that the digitisation and preservation of village, *nagrik* (residents) and land records in the district are essential to carry forward the ancestral searches. With easily accessible records, roots seekers would have the satisfaction of locating the home village or the particular region that was part of their origins even if there are no relatives living in the ancestral village.

Christelle Gourdine, a French national of Guadeloupe and Indian origin had long been fascinated by her Indian heritage. Born in the south of France, Christelle was often asked where she came from. "People (in France) are surprised when I reply that I am from Guadeloupe."

Christelle tried to learn about her family's origins. Her parents had moved from Guadeloupe, a French territory in the Caribbean to France. "My family left India between 1860 and 1885 but I've never found any documents at home or at the Archives about them. On my father's side, my ancestor named Gourdine s/o Bachou was from North India and on my mother's side, my ancestor named Moutou s/o Vaitilingom was from the Madras Presidency," she said. It meant her ancestors were 'Calcuttans', the name given within the Indian community in Guadeloupe to workers who came from Calcutta port.

Christelle Gourdine considers herself a Frenchwoman but talks about the "irresistible" link with India. On her first visit to India, she felt immediately at home though she could not speak any Indian language. "It was the first time in my life that no one looked at me because I stood out due to my ethnicity. It's our home; our DNA still vibrates in India," she said. It brings her back to India again and again. "I have been to India 14 times since my first visit to the country six years ago," she noted.

Christelle travelled through India researching indenture documents in Kolkata, Delhi, Lucknow and Chennai. She was deeply disappointed when she could not find any links to her ancestors in India despite travelling to so many places. "I was very frustrated, almost in despair about my research, so I went to Varanasi to take a break. I spent a week there, and then performed a last ritual for my ancestors. Just before leaving, I took a dip in the Ganga at the opposite side of the main *ghat* and had an intensely emotional moment – it changed the way I felt. I felt an intense relief; I felt my mission for my ancestors was accomplished. It made a profound and lasting impression on me. I had not been able to find their original homes but I felt as though I had somehow connected with them," Christelle explained.

Many other people of Indian descent just want to travel to India and visit the places associated with their ancestors' odyssey to a new land. Gail Samlalsingh sent an email, saying: "My husband Vishnu and I will be going to India in January with a desire to walk in some of the places where our original relatives walked. We have no 'root names' as mentioned in your article but would still like to go and discover and observe. We are originally from Trinidad but live in Toronto now." The Samlalsinghs travelled through India visiting the tourist destinations and pilgrimage sites to get a feel of India. But it was the newly inaugurated Memorial to the Indentured Emigrants in Kolkata that was the most memorable and natural place of pilgrimage for the couple.

The Indenture Memorial, which was inaugurated in January 2011 is located at the Kidderpore Depot at 14 Garden Reach along the banks of the Hoogly River. The site of the memorial is next to an old clock tower near the Demerara jetty. Each recruiting colony had a depot where the recruits were housed till they were ready to board the ship. The recruits walked down to the jetty to the small boats that carried them to the huge ocean going ships.

Steeped in the history of indenture recruitment, the memorial creates an emotional resonance for the visitors to the site. It has a special meaning for the descendents of the Indians migrants – it is the place from where the actual journey abroad and the experience of indentureship began. It was the point of no return from where thousands of indentured emigrants left the various jetties along the Hoogly River to board the ships that would take them to their destinations.

The inscription on the commemorative plaque on the memorial states: "In honoured tribute to Indian Indentured labourers – With due recognition and lasting remembrance of Indian indentured labourers who left these shores during the 19th and 20th centuries, seeking better livelihoods in far away lands, for their pioneering spirit, determination, resilience, endurance, perseverance and sacrifices amidst extremely harsh conditions. For their invaluable contributions to lands they adopted, and for the triumph of the spirit of Indianness they maintained and passed on to their descendants."

A second phase of the memorial project is being planned as a public project to set up a museum that would be a repository of the history of indenture. It involves setting up a heritage museum cum resource centre that would house records of the Indian indentured migration, individual emigration records, data on the migration, conditions on the plantations, books, photographs, documentaries and literature of the diaspora.

There is a growing desire among the *pravasi* Indians to develop a deeper and richer knowledge of family history and explore their cultural heritage. Stories, myths and memories of a homeland lurk somewhere in the subconscious, most of them assimilated at different times in one's life; they get triggered off by a variety of stimuli at a receptive period and grow into a burning desire to know more about one's origins. For most of them it is a deeply felt emotional desire to know where their ancestors came from, a nostalgic yearning to learn something about their forefathers lives.

Their dream is to locate the region, the village where their ancestors were born and then to try and trace relatives in India. If that is not possible to visit the old home, then a simple reconnecting with India and their Indianness becomes a deeply rewarding experience for people like Christelle Gourdine and the Samlalsinghs. More and more overseas Indians have come to believe that it is important for them to learn and understand their own stories and then pass them on from one generation to the other. It is the stories that link individuals to their past and gives them a sense of identity.